WHOM SAY YE THAT I AM?

MITCHELL C. TAYLOR

CFI
An imprint of Cedar Fort, Inc.
Springville, Utah

© 2025 Mitchell C. Taylor
All rights reserved.

No part of this book may be reproduced in any form whatsoever, whether by graphic, visual, electronic, film, microfilm, tape recording, or any other means, without prior written permission of the publisher, except in the case of brief passages embodied in critical reviews and articles.

This is not an official publication of The Church of Jesus Christ of Latter-day Saints. The opinions and views expressed herein belong solely to the author and do not necessarily represent the opinions or views of Cedar Fort, Inc. Permission for the use of sources, graphics, and photos is also solely the responsibility of the author.

Paperback ISBN 13: 978-1-4621-4847-9
eBook ISBN 13: 978-1-4621-4848-6

Published by CFI, an imprint of Cedar Fort, Inc.
2373 W. 700 S., Suite 100, Springville, UT 84663
Distributed by Cedar Fort, Inc., www.cedarfort.com

Library of Congress Control Number: 2024945237

Cover design by Shawnda Craig
Cover design © 2025 Cedar Fort, Inc.
Edited by Evelyn Coleman

Printed in the United States of America

10 9 8 7 6 5 4 3 2 1

Printed on acid-free paper

To my mom, whose unwavering faith in Jesus has been a guiding light in my life. Your example of love and service inspires me. I thank God for blessing me with such a wonderful mother. This book is dedicated to you with gratitude and admiration. I love you, Mom.

Contents

Preface xi
Do You Know Jesus? 1
The Names of Jesus 7
    Advocate 8
    Almighty 9
    Alpha and Omega 10
    Amen 11
    Apostle 12
    Author and Finisher of Our Faith 13
    Beloved 14
    Bread of Life 15
    Bridegroom 17
    Bright and Morning Star 19
    Captain of Salvation 20
    Carpenter 21
    Chief Cornerstone 22
    Christ, Messiah 23
    Commander, Leader 25
    Confidence 26
    Counselor 28
    Creator 30
    Deliverer 31

Door	32
El Shaddai	33
El Simkhat Gili	34
The Everlasting Father	36
Exemplar	37
Firstborn	38
Friend of Sinners	39
Gift	42
God	43
Good Shepherd	44
Governor	46
Grace	48
Great High Priest	50
Greater	51
Holy, Holy, Holy	53
Hope	54
I AM	55
Immanuel	57
Jesus	58
Jesus of Nazareth, Nazarene	59
Judge	60
Keeper of the Gate	62
King	63
Lamb of God	65
Lawgiver	66
Light of the World	68
Lion of the Tribe of Judah	69
Lord	70
Lord of Hosts	71
Lord of the Sabbath	72
Man of Sorrows	74

Master	75
Mediator	76
Meek and Lowly	77
The Mighty God	79
Omnipotent	80
One	81
Our Passover	82
Perfection	84
Physician	86
Potter	88
The Prince of Peace	89
Prophet	90
Rabbi and Rabboni	91
Redeemer	93
Rest	95
The Resurrection and the Life	96
Righteous Branch	98
Rock	99
Savior and Salvation	101
Strength	103
Sure Foundation	104
True Vine	106
Witness	108
Wonderful	110
Word	111

Conclusion: Remember Who You Are	113
Endnotes	120
About the Author	133

Preface

I have referenced thirty-six different Bible translations throughout this book. I believe there is value in this for three reasons.

First, the study of various Bible translations can give further insight to the meaning of the Bible's original text. I served a mission in Honduras and learned the Spanish language. When translating from one language to another, important meanings can easily be lost or changed. Just as meaning can be lost or changed going from Spanish to English or English to Spanish, so, too, can meaning be lost or changed when the original Biblical languages of Hebrew, Aramaic, and Greek are translated to English. Looking at the Hebrew, Aramaic, and Greek words of the Bible, along with various English translations, can help us better understand the scriptures.

For example, the King James Version of Exodus 20:13 reads, "Thou shalt not kill." This translation would appear to exclude all killing, including self-defense and war. In Hebrew, the word that means all forms of killing is the word *harag*. However, the Hebrew word used in Exodus 20:13 is *ratsah*, which refers to acts of criminal killing. A more accurate translation of Exodus 20:13 would be, "Thou shalt not murder."[1] The New International Version, New Living Translation, English Standard Version, New American Standard Bible, and many others translate Exodus 20:13 to be "Thou shalt not murder" instead of "Thou shalt not kill." Looking at these translations provides greater understanding of the original Hebrew text.

The second reason for utilizing different Bible translations is to illustrate the variety of meanings contained in the original Hebrew and Greek words. Like English, Hebrew & Greek have words with multiple or layered meanings. It's not always possible to grasp the depth of a biblical word with a single English translation. Looking at different English translations helps us better understand the original Greek and Hebrew text and the gospel of Jesus Christ.

For example, when I was learning Spanish as a missionary, I learned that the word *fresa* means strawberry. However, one day while I was walking down the street, I heard people talking about *fresas*, but I didn't see any *fresas*. Confused, I asked my companion and he explained to me that *fresa* does mean strawberry, but in some instances, it can also refer to a person who is elegant and flaunts their riches. Just as I misunderstood the word *fresa* in Spanish, sometimes translators of the Bible use an incorrect definition of a Hebrew, Greek, or Aramaic word when translating to English. For example, the Greek word *airo* has multiple meanings. *Airo* can mean "take away or cut off," but it also can mean "to lift, raise, take up, to lift up."[2] There are times in English Bible translations that translators use the wrong meaning of the word *airo* and translate the word as "take away or cut off" when a more correct translation would be "lift up." Using the words "take away or cut off" instead of "lift up" significantly changes the meaning and understanding of a Bible verse. Reading and studying other Bible translations can help us better understand the original meanings, enriching our faith in Christ and His gospel.

The third reason I use different translations of the Bible is because viewing other translations can help us see a familiar scripture in a new light, revealing a deeper or alternative meaning. We may think we know what a verse is saying because we have heard it many times. A new translation of a familiar scripture can be a catalyst for deeper thought and understanding.

Just as misunderstanding of the Hebrew, Aramaic, and Greek can change our understanding of the Bible so too can misunderstandings about grace affect our understanding of the scriptures and the gospel.

Understanding Grace

The grace of Jesus Christ is at the center of His gospel and yet grace is often misunderstood. The scriptures continually teach us that it is only in and through the Lord Jesus Christ and His grace that we are saved. To understand and receive the good news that is found within each of the names of the Lord Jesus Christ, we must understand grace. The key to understanding grace is understanding the doctrines of justification and sanctification.

Justification and Sanctification

"We know that justification through the grace of our Lord and Savior Jesus Christ is just and true. We know also, that sanctification through the grace of our Lord and Savior Jesus Christ is just and true" (Doctrine and Covenants 20:30-31).

To better understand the doctrines of justification and sanctification, I would like to share an analogy I call the pit of sin. Pretend for a moment that you have fallen into a pit that is a mile deep. You try to climb the walls, but it's impossible. The walls of the pit go straight up and there is nothing to hold on to. You try jumping. You try climbing. You try digging. Each attempt you make to climb the wall results in the same outcome. You're falling back to the bottom of the pit.

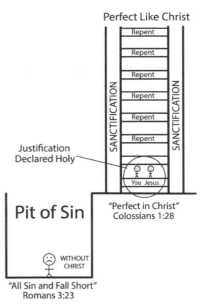

As a result of the fall of Adam, we have all sinned and thus fall short of the perfection required to be in the presence of God. Spiritually, we have each fallen into the equivalent of a mile-deep pit. We try as hard as we can to overcome our fallen natures and to get right with God. We try to keep all the commandments, but since we inevitably fail, we then try to make it up to God by increasing our good works quota, hoping maybe these actions will sway the judgment of God in our favor. We hope somehow if our good works outweigh our sins, we will be able to get right with God. The bad news, though, is even after all our disciplined efforts and our countless good works, we are still far from being perfect, and we are thus unable to escape the pit of sin.

As we begin to realize the futility of our situation, and that it is truly impossible to get ourselves out of this spiritual pit, we fall into despair.

We so badly want to escape. All our attempts lead us to a vital moment in which we turn to God and say as did the publican, "God be merciful to me a sinner."[3] We change from being confident in our own efforts to a state in which we leave it to God and recognize our total dependence upon Him.

As we glance up, we see Christ, arms outstretched, calling us by name. We cry out, "Lord, save me!"[4] Christ grabs us, pulling us out of the pit of sin, freeing us from its grasp.

When Christ frees us from the pit, this is called justification: declaring sinners perfect in Christ and holy even though there still is a gap between our performance and perfection. The gift of justification is instant when we put our faith and trust in Christ. Once we have entered this saving relationship of being perfect in Christ, we then begin the process of sanctification, becoming perfect like Christ.

When Christ frees us from the pit of sin, we are instantly *perfect in Him*, but we are not instantly *perfect like Him*. Attaining complete obedience through Christ (sanctification) is a lengthy process. There are no shortcuts. Once we have escaped the pit of sin and are declared perfect in Christ, Christ leads us up the ladder of sanctification. Climbing this sanctification ladder is the process of becoming perfect like Christ. Our ascent up the ladder will often be slow, and at times we will fail and fall a few rungs. During these times, though, Christ will be there to catch us and help us begin our climb again. As we climb, we can have a perfect assurance that although we are not perfect like Christ, we are still perfect in Christ.

The true doctrine of justification by grace does not lead to moral irresponsibility, laziness, passivity, or disobedience. True justification will never lead a man to more sin but will instead lead to fuller repentance and obedience. If you don't desire obedience (notice I have said desire, not that you are actually obedient), you haven't truly entered the covenant which justifies.

After All We Can Do

Some common misconceptions on grace comes from a misunderstanding of 2 Nephi 25:23, "For we labor diligently to write, to persuade our children, and also our brethren, to believe in Christ, and to be reconciled to God; for we know that it is by grace that we are saved, after all we can do."

Elder Dieter F Uchtdorf taught, "I wonder if sometimes we misinterpret the phrase 'after all we can do.' We must understand that 'after' does not equal 'because.' We are not saved 'because' of all that we can do. Have any of us done *all* that we can do? Does God wait until we've expended every effort before He will intervene in our lives with His saving grace?"[5]

We can never do all we can do, which is precisely why we need a Savior in the first place. Making everything we could have done the requirement to receive grace defeats the entire point of sending a Savior. Christ isn't a lifeguard waiting to throw the life preserver after we have expended our last effort to save ourselves. He saves us from the depths of sin as soon as we turn to Him.

While justification (becoming perfect in Christ) is instantaneous, sanctification (becoming perfect like Christ) is progressive. There is work to be done to become perfect like Christ. We can't magically declare, "I want to be a heart surgeon" and become one. It takes work. Likewise, becoming like Christ requires work. Since works are required to become like Christ, some erroneously jump to the conclusion that our works do part of the saving. Works are required and essential, but they don't do the saving. Mosiah 3:17 declares, "And moreover, I say unto you, that there shall be no other name given nor any other way nor means whereby salvation can come unto the children of men, only in and through the name of Christ, the Lord Omnipotent." There is no other name given. Not mine. Not yours. The only name by which we are saved is Jesus. Jesus does 100 percent of the saving.

So, what is grace?

BYU held an event to discuss grace and celebrate the twenty-fifth anniversary of the publication of the book *Believing Christ* by Dr. Stephen E. Robinson, at which, he was asked to speak. At the conclusion of his remarks, Dr. Robinson shared the following definition of grace.

> I'm sure you've heard definitions of grace until they are coming out of your ears today. I don't like theological definitions . . . So when my students ask me, 'What is grace?' I answer with an analogy. Generally, there is someone in my class who just had a baby.

And I ask them to stand up and I ask them, "When they put that child in your arms for the first time, what were your feelings?"

"Overwhelming love."

"Why? What had that child done to earn that?"

"Nothing. It just was. It just got born and it's mine."

That's grace. We belong to heavenly parents into whose arms we were put at some point—who would do anything in their power to exalt us in their kingdom. The one hang up is we have agency. And sometimes we won't cooperate. But grace is that preexisting disposition on the part of our heavenly parents, our brother Jesus Christ, to do anything that can be done. And that's a lot—to get us to our exaltation—if we will just cooperate. Do you want to know what grace is? Go find a newborn baby and hang on to it for a minute and ask yourself what your feelings are.[6]

This is grace.

Each of the names of Jesus contained in this book are a powerful witness of His grace and His gifts of salvation and eternal life.

Do You Know Jesus?

Who do you say that I am?
-Jesus (Matthew 16:15, Amplified Bible, Classic Edition)

While on the earth, Jesus proposed a question to His apostles saying, "Whom do men say that I am?"[7] With confidence, His apostles answered, "John the Baptist . . . some say Elias; and others, One of the prophets."[8] He then asked them the most important question, "But whom say ye that I am?"[9]

We must ask ourselves: Who is Jesus? Is He the Christ or a good teacher? Is He the Son of God or a lunatic? Is He resurrected, or was His body stolen? While we can listen to other testimonies and hear their witness of Jesus, the only way to come to our own conclusion is by desiring to know.

We need to study, pray, and seek to come to understand who Jesus truly is. You can't just ask, "Jesus, are you the Christ?" and do nothing. Is that how you make friends? Do you just walk up to a random stranger and ask them to be your friend? If you tried this, you would instantly be turned down. If you want to be friends with someone, you have to be genuinely interested in the person. You need to get to know them by asking questions, hanging out, laughing together, and crying together.

The way we create relationships with others is the way Jesus wants us to come unto Him. He wants us to get to know Him just as He knows each one of us. He wants you to ask questions. He wants you to take time to be with Him. He wants you to come to Him with your pains and concerns. He wants you to intimately know Him just as He knows you.

Mitchell C. Taylor

He Knows You!

Jesus doesn't just know *about* you. He knows *you*. He knows your pains, sorrows, and weaknesses. Jesus suffered in Gethsemane and on the cross so He could know every little thing about you. If Jesus was willing to die so He could know you, shouldn't we give Him a couple minutes of our day to come to know Him? Jeremiah 29:13 teaches, "You will seek Me and find Me when you search for Me with all your heart."[10] If you seek Jesus, you will find Him, and you will personally come to know Him. Jesus declares, "Do not fear, for I have redeemed you; I have called you by name; you are Mine!"[11] Jesus has redeemed you so He could call you His own. He wants *you!*

The One Thing We Cannot Say

While Jesus has given everything to know us, some will say Jesus is a great person, but not the Son of God. To people who say, "I'm ready to accept Jesus as a great moral teacher, but I don't accept His claim to be God," C. S. Lewis taught, "That is the one thing we must not say. A man who was merely a man and said the sort of things Jesus said would not be a great moral teacher. He would either be a lunatic—on the level with the man who says he is a poached egg—or else he would be the Devil of Hell. You must make your choice. Either this man was, and is, the Son of God, or else a madman or something worse. You can shut him up for a fool, you can spit at him and kill him as a demon or you can fall at his feet and call him Lord and God, but let us not come with any patronizing nonsense about his being a great human teacher. He has not left that open to us. He did not intend to."[12]

Jesus has made the decision simple. Either He is the Christ or a madman. We cannot say He is an outstanding teacher but not the Christ or we will receive the rebuke, "You know me not."[13]

How Can I Know?

Thomas was a great apostle of the Lord Jesus Christ, but like all of us, he had doubts and questions. After Jesus talked with the apostles, Thomas asked, "How can we know?"[14] We all have asked this question. We want to know, but how? There is only one way to come to know—the Holy

Ghost. 1 Corinthians 12:3 states, "No one can say, 'Jesus is Lord,' except by the Holy Spirit."[15] Jesus enthusiastically told Peter, "God has blessed you, Simon, son of Jonah . . . for my Father in heaven has personally revealed this to you—this is not from any human source."[16]

It is only "by the power of the Holy Ghost ye may know"[17] that Jesus is the Christ. If you want to know Jesus, pray, read, and seek. As you actively seek, the Lord will tell you with joy just as He told Peter, "Blessed art thou, [insert your name], for flesh and blood hath not revealed it unto thee, but my Father which is in heaven."[18] If you have a desire to come to know Jesus, the Spirit will confirm that He is the Christ, and you will be able to declare like Peter, "[I] believe and know that you are The Messiah, The Son of the living God."[19]

You're Not Your Tone of Voice

I served as a missionary for The Church of Jesus Christ of Latter-Day Saints in Honduras for two years. I love Jesus Christ and I am very passionate about His gospel. I love to teach and share messages with everyone. Sadly, however, my passion can be confused for anger. People sometimes asked me, "Are you mad?" or "Did I say something that made you mad?" Not coming across as angry is something I have been working on my whole life.

One day, after getting back from an exchange with the assistants to the mission president, my companion told me that many people mentioned to him that they had been offended because I had gotten angry with them. One of the ladies exclaimed to him, "How can he be a missionary if he gets angry with people?"

After hearing these comments, I beat myself up. I felt so inadequate. I muttered to myself, "People misunderstood the point of the message because of my tone of voice." As I was chewing myself out, the Lord brought to my mind the following, "You're not your tone of voice. You are my son, my faithful disciple, and defender of the faith."

Like me, all of us have weaknesses and make mistakes. Christ taught, "I give men weakness that they may be humble"[20] Christ gives us weaknesses so we put our trust in Him. However, Satan will use our weaknesses to define us and make us feel inadequate. Satan wants to constantly remind us of our weaknesses, our "tone of voice." He will tell us that nobody loves us because of our weaknesses. He will trick us into believing we *are* our "tone of voice."

We all are sinners and fall short of the glory of God (Romans 3:23). However, Jesus doesn't define us by this. He doesn't call us by our weaknesses. He defines you by who He is. He calls us His children. He calls us loved. He calls us redeemed. He calls us His. Jesus doesn't define you by your past. He views you as what you can become. Satan focuses on our sins while Christ views our potential. Don't listen to Satan. Listen to Christ and what He calls you.

I Will Give You a New Name

You will have a new name that the Lord himself will give you.
Isaiah 62:2, Easy-to-Read Version

Jesus gives us a far greater name than we could ever imagine. Jesus promises, "I will give them—within the walls of my house—a memorial and a name far greater than sons and daughters could give. For the name I give them is an everlasting one. It will never disappear!"[21] He gives us His perfect name that will never go away.

When we enter a covenant relationship with Jesus through the waters of baptism, we take upon ourselves the name of Christ. We are called by a "new name"[22]—His name. And even though we are sinners, we are justified by our covenant relationship and declared perfect in Christ. Satan calls us sinners, but Jesus calls us saints. Satan calls us guilty, lost, and hopeless, but Jesus calls us righteous, redeemed, and reborn.

When we enter a covenant relationship with Jesus, His names become our names. We still sin but are now defined by the Sinless One. Even though you are a sinner, the title of "sinner" no longer defines you. Jesus defines you, and He will call you spotless before Him. Jesus "doth call you; yea, and in his own name he doth call you, which is the name of Christ."[23]

Do You Know the Name by Which You Are Called?

Jesus's name sets us free. John 8:32 declares, "And you will know the truth, and the truth will set you free."[24] The truth is a name for Christ. If you substitute Jesus's name for truth, we read, "And you will know [Jesus], and [Jesus] will set you free." Acts 4:12 declares, "for there is no other name under heaven given among men by which we must be saved."[25] The name of Jesus saves you.

The way we gain eternal life is by having a relationship with God and understanding our dependence on Him. John 17:3 teaches, "And this is the way to have eternal life—to know you, the only true God, and Jesus Christ, the one you sent to earth."[26] Studying the names of Jesus will help you come to know Jesus and His divine role in your life. It will help you put your full trust in Him.

Jeffrey R. Holland, an apostle of the Lord Jesus Christ, teaches, "In our search 'to know . . . God, and Jesus Christ, whom [He] hast sent' (John 17:3), we can learn more about who Christ was, is, and will yet be by examining the names and titles given to Him than by any other method."[27]

The best way to come to know Jesus is to study His names. "He reveals himself through His designations, and all His glorious names meet varying needs in our own lives. They reveal diverse dimensions of His power, love, grace, glory, and goodness that touch our souls. They disclose the many layers of His relationship with us. His names help us fix our thoughts on Him in new ways. They fill our minds with Him who can fill our hearts and guide our lives. Each of His names helps reassure us of His love in so many different ways."[28] As you study the names of Jesus, you will also learn the many new names He gives you. In Him, we find our worth and identity. Mosiah 5:9 declares, "Whosoever doeth this shall be found at the right hand of God, for he shall know the name by which he is called; for he shall be called by the name of Christ."

As you read, I hope you can come to know the name by which you are called and cement your answer to the question Jesus asked His disciples, "Whom say ye that I am?"[29]

The Names of Jesus

Remember the Lord, who is great and awesome.
Nehemiah 4:14, New International Version

"There is one name that recalls a quality of the Master that bewildered and compelled those who knew him. It reveals a side of him that, when recognized, is enough to make you fall on your face . . . [the name of] Jesus. In the four gospels of the New Testament, it's His most common name—used almost six hundred times . . . A name so typical, if He were here today, His name might be John or Bob or Jim. He was touchable, approachable, reachable . . . 'Just call me Jesus,' you can almost hear Him say. He was the kind of fellow you'd invite to watch the football game at your house. He'd wrestle on the floor with your kids, doze on your couch, and cook steaks on your grill. He'd laugh at your jokes and tell a few of His own. And when you spoke, He'd listen to you as if He had all the time in eternity . . . Those who walked with Him remembered Him not with a title or designation, but with a name—Jesus . . . It's a beautiful name and a powerful name."[30]

For this reason, the most frequent name we use throughout this book to refer to the Creator of the Universe is Jesus!

Philippians 2:10-11 prophesies that the day is coming when "At the name of Jesus every knee will bow . . . and that every tongue will confess that Jesus is the Lord."[31]

Mitchell C. Taylor

Advocate

If any man sin, we have an advocate with the father, Jesus Christ the righteous.
1 John 2:1, King James Version

If you were in court, would you prefer an attorney who wins some of the time or an attorney who has never lost a case? We desire to be pronounced "not guilty" in the sight of God so we can return to live with Him, but we are in a predicament. We all "have sinned and fall short of the glory of God."[32]

If we are judged by the law, we are declared guilty and "consigned to a state of endless misery and woe."[33] How can we be saved from this awful judgment? We need someone to plead on our behalf and declare us "not guilty."

Thankfully, we have the greatest advocate in the universe at our side—Jesus. Romans 8:1 reads, "Therefore, there is now no condemnation for those who are in Christ Jesus who walk not after the flesh, but after the Spirit."[34] With Jesus, we are guaranteed victory.

In Greek, the word 'advocate' is *parakleton,* which means advisor, helper, called to aid, to console, to enrich and strengthen. Without Jesus as our advocate, we are all spiritually dead, but "God wiped out the charges that were against us for disobeying the Law . . . He took them away and nailed them to the cross."[35] Jesus has paid the price for our sins. Jesus took our "guilty" verdict upon Himself so we can receive a "not-guilty" verdict.

Even though we are sinners, Jesus doesn't condemn us if we believe in Him.[36] The law seeks to declare our guilt, but Jesus has satisfied the demands of the law. He can say to each of us as He did the woman taken in adultery, "Where are those thine accusers? Hath no man condemned thee? . . . Neither do I condemn thee."[37]

We all have violated God's laws, and without an advocate, we are guilty. We can try to plead our own case, but no matter how hard we try on our own, we still will be declared guilty. Jesus has paid the price for our sins, and He rushes to our aid as our advocate. Jesus pleads on our behalf saying, "I know this one has sinned and has violated our commands. She is guilty. However, My sacrifice satisfies the debt she owes. My righteousness was applied to her account when she trusted in Me for salvation. I have paid her debt. She has no debt! She must be pronounced not guilty!"

The Doctrine and Covenants records these words of the Savior, "Listen to him who is the advocate with the Father, who is pleading your cause before him— Saying: Father, behold the sufferings and death of him who did no sin, in whom thou wast well pleased; behold the blood of thy Son which was shed, the blood of him whom thou gavest that thyself might be glorified; Wherefore, Father, spare these my brethren that believe on my name, that they may come unto me and have everlasting life."[38]

Through our advocate with the Father, Jesus, we are saved. When we are in a relationship with Jesus, we have no need to fear whether we will be pronounced guilty. Jesus has satisfied the demands of justice and settled our case. We are not guilty!

Jesus's name is Advocate. Your new name is **triumphant**. When you are with Jesus, you can't lose. You can have confidence in "the triumph and the glory of the Lamb, who was slain."[39] You will "always . . . triumph in Christ."[40]

Almighty

I will be your Father, and you will be my sons and daughters, says the LORD Almighty.
2 Corinthians 6:18, New Living Translation

Have you ever wondered what it would be like to have superpowers? You could fly, have super speed, and even insane strength. This would be awesome, but sadly, we are finite humans with no superpowers. However, we have a friend who is a superhero with all powers. He is Almighty.

Christ came to earth as a man to save us. However, He was no ordinary man. He came with the power of God. The powers of sin and death were no match for Jesus. He paid our debts in Gethsemane and on the cross so we could be forgiven. He left His tomb empty on that wondrous Easter morning so we could be resurrected. Jesus used His Almighty powers to save us.

Job 9:10 says of Jesus, "He performs wonders that cannot be fathomed, miracles that cannot be counted."[41] We shouldn't put our faith and trust in anyone or anything other than the Almighty God and His son. Christ has fought our battles. He has delivered us from sin and death. He is Almighty.

"Moses was caught up into an exceedingly high mountain, and he saw God face to face, and he talked with him, and the glory of God was upon Moses . . . And God spake unto Moses, saying: Behold, I am the Lord God Almighty."[42] Following this experience, Moses said, "I know that man is nothing, which thing I never had supposed."[43] Compared to God we are nothing, and "[we] cannot say that [we] are even as much as the dust of the earth."[44]

On our own, we can "do nothing,"[45] but with the Almighty God we can move mountains and do the impossible.[46] "Nothing is too hard for [God]."[47]

Jesus is Almighty. Your new name is **strong**. "The Lord is [your] strength."[48] You can say as did the apostle Paul, "I can do all things through Christ who strengthens me."[49] "With God nothing will be impossible."[50]

Alpha and Omega

I am Alpha and Omega, the beginning and the end.
3 Nephi 9:18

Alpha and Omega are the first and last letters of the Greek alphabet. Jesus saying, "I am Alpha and Omega," is the equivalent of Him saying, "I am A to Z." Jesus is the beginning and the end and everything in between.

Sometimes we might take the alphabet for granted and not fully realize its critical role in our lives. Without the alphabet, we wouldn't be able to spell words or communicate with friends. Life would be a mess.

Jesus is the whole alphabet. Without Him, all is chaos. We cannot overlook Jesus's central role in our lives. In general conference, Ryan K. Olson said, "No matter how difficult or confusing the challenges may be, you can always remember that the answer is simple: it is always Jesus."[51]

Whom Say Ye that I Am?

Jesus is the beginning and the end of our salvation. Jesus is every word and every letter. There is no other alphabet that spells out our salvation. Salvation is only found in the name of J-E-S-U-S. "It is finished; it is finished! The Lamb of God hath overcome and trodden the wine press alone."[52]

Jesus is also the Alpha and Omega of creation. All creation begins and ends with Jesus. He created the world.[53] He created us in His image.[54] All things are done through Jesus by command of the Father.[55]

Jesus is our God from the beginning to the end. He never leaves us. He is with us at the start, at the finish, and at all the times in between. He is with us when we are up, and He is with us when we are down. He is with us when we succeed, and He is with us when we fail. He is with us when we are faithful, and He is with us when we betray him. He is with us when we resist temptation, and He is with us when we sin. He is with us when we are strong, and He is with us when we are weak.

Jesus's name is Alpha and Omega. Your new name is **eternal**. Jesus is everlasting and there is no end to those who have Jesus with them. He is your Savior "even unto the end."[56]

Amen

These things saith the Amen, the faithful and true witness, the beginning of the creation.
Revelation 3:14, King James Version

We all are very familiar with the word 'amen'. We say it at the end of every prayer. However, since we use 'amen' so often, much of its true meaning has been lost. It has just become the word we say at the end of each prayer. In Hebrew, 'amen' means firm, steadfast, or let it be as has been said. When we say 'amen', we affirm that we believe God will answer this prayer.

When we declare 'amen,' we are yielding to the will of the Father as did Jesus. When Christ was in the garden, He cried to His Father saying, "Abba, Father, all things are possible for you. Remove this cup from me. Yet not what I will, but what you will."[57]

Whatever Heavenly Father commands, Jesus does. Jesus is the true and faithful one of the Father. "For all the promises of God in him are yea, and in him Amen, unto the glory of God by us."[58] We say 'amen' to align our wills with the will of the Father. We say 'amen' to give all glory to God. We say 'amen' because we believe God will fulfill all His promises. For we know that whatever He says will come to pass for God cannot lie.[59]

'Amen' was also commonly used in a legal sense. 'Amen' represented two parties agreeing on something. The parties debated until both were satisfied. The judge gave the amen, and it was settled.

Jesus is the Amen that satisfies the demands of justice. The law demands justice and wants us to be punished. Jesus paid the price to satisfy the law. The law receives justice, and we receive mercy, grace, and forgiveness. Both parties are satisfied. The judge gives the Amen, and it is settled.

Jesus is our Amen for salvation. He has redeemed our souls from hell. He agreed with the law to take all our pains, sins, and judgments. Every time we hear the word Amen, we should remember and thank our Savior, for Amen is His name.

Jesus often repeats the words, "Ask and ye shall receive." Saying 'amen' at the end of your prayer is an act of faith. It is a statement of assurance that God will answer. Jesus encourages us to pray with faith, hope, and assurance saying, "When you pray and ask for something, believe that you have received it, and you will be given whatever you ask for."[60]

Jesus's name is Amen. Your new name is **answered.** "All things you ask in prayer, believing, you will receive . . . Ask and it will be given to you."[61]

Apostle

Wherefore, holy brethren, partakers of the heavenly calling, consider the Apostle . . . of our profession, Christ Jesus.
Hebrews 3:1, King James Version

If we say, "Jesus the apostle," it doesn't sound right. Jesus isn't an apostle. Right? When we hear "apostle," our thoughts are most likely of a member of the quorum of the twelve apostles. While these twelve are indeed the Lord's ordained servants, there is only one chief and great Apostle—even the Lord Jesus Christ.

An apostle is someone sent by someone else, having a particular mission with sufficient power to accomplish the mission. Jesus was sent by His Father to complete a mission, and He had the power to accomplish it. His mission was to reconcile us to God. He suffered and died to unlock the chains of death and hell. Jesus is the One that Heavenly Father sent to save us all.

The Greek word for apostle is *apostellein*, which means to send out. In Hebrew, apostle, *shaliach*, means representative, to envoy. Jesus told His apostles, "As the Father hath sent me, even so send I you."[62] The quorum of the twelve apostles are representatives and mouthpieces of the Lord. Doctrine and Covenants 1:38 declares, "Whether by mine own voice or by the voice of my servants, it is the same." The apostles are special witnesses of the Lord Jesus Christ.

Likewise, Jesus is the Apostle, envoy or *shaliach* of God. Jesus is the messenger of the covenant. His mission is to lead us to salvation and eternal life. He was sent by God to give us the way to return to live with our Heavenly Father. He is the messenger of the good news. He *is* the good news!

Jesus's name is Apostle. Your new name is **witness**. Like the apostles, you can "declare [your] allegiance to God"[63] and share the good news of Jesus with others.

Author and Finisher of Our Faith

[Look] unto Jesus the author and finisher of our faith.
Hebrews 12:2, King James Version

When I started writing my first book, I constantly wanted to give up. Writing can be a difficult and tedious process. You have to write, rewrite, and edit until your brain hurts. At times I wanted to stop writing, but I knew I had to keep going because the Lord asked me to. Whenever I thought of giving up, I remembered the promise of Nephi, "For I know that the Lord giveth no commandments unto the children of men, save he shall prepare a way for them that they may accomplish the thing which he commandeth them."[64]

There is someone who will never give up on you regardless of how hard it gets—Jesus. He is the author and finisher of your faith. He started us, and He will finish us. He will never quit on us.

The word 'author' means to create and perfect. Jesus is our author—our creator. He knows us better than we know ourselves. If you need to know how to use an invention, who better to ask than the inventor.

Jesus is our author, creator, and inventor, but He doesn't stop there. He is also the finisher. He created us to become like Him. We need to trust Him to finish us. He is beside us, helping us become more like Him until we are perfect.

We are all a work in progress. We won't be perfect in this life, but eventually, through the grace of our Lord and Savior, we will be perfect like Him. Trust in the Lord to finish the job. If we trust in Him, desiring to become like him, eventually we will hear the voice of the Lord say, "[You are] finished."[65]

Jesus's name is Author and Finisher of your faith. Your new name is **wanted.** Jesus will never give up on you. You are His work and His glory.[66]

Beloved

This is my Beloved Son: Hear him.
Luke 9:35, King James Version

In Greek mythology, there is a story about a god name Eros who falls in love with a mortal named Psyche. In the story, Psyche and Eros are talking. Psyche wishes to know who her husband is. At this point in the story, Psyche isn't allowed to see Eros or know his name. She has no idea she is married to a God. She has been calling him "Nobody" but wants to call him by a new name. She decides on a new name, saying, "I shall call you Beloved because you are my beloved."

When someone or something is called "beloved," it means greatly loved or dear to the heart. Every time Heavenly Father introduces Jesus Christ, He declares, "This is my beloved son."[67] When I first saw this meaning, I thought, *Doesn't God love us all greatly? Why is Christ the beloved Son? Aren't we all beloved?*

As I did more research, I found a very powerful symbolism in words that begin with "be." When "be" begins a word, it means completely, thoroughly, fully. Examples are:

Be + get = to fully deliver.

Be + low = completely underneath.

Be + loved = fully, thoroughly, and completely loved.

We all are loved sons and daughters of God but Jesus is the Beloved Son. He fully and completely followed the will of the Father. He fully atoned for our sins. Jesus is the Beloved Son since He fully and completely obeys the Father.

This name Beloved Son is also given as a title of kingship and designation. Jesus has fully pleased God with His sinless life and perfect obedience. Heavenly Father perfectly loves us and holds us dear to His heart, but none of us have fully obeyed the Father and been perfect in all things.

Jesus's name is Beloved. Your new name is **loved**. Your Heavenly Father loves you unconditionally. He loves you so much He sent His Beloved Son to die for you. "For God so loved the world that he gave his only begotten son, that whosoever believeth in him should not perish but have everlasting life."[68]

Bread of Life

"I am the bread of life: he that cometh to me shall never hunger."[69]
—Jesus (John 6:35 King James Version)

We know fasting is a good thing, but fasting can be painful. It can feel like you are literally starving yourself. Some fast Sundays I am tempted to ransack the pantry to satisfy my hunger.

We fast to show our love for God, but as humans we need food to survive. If we don't eat, we die. This is why Jesus compares Himself to bread, a common source of food. If we don't have Jesus, we die. An old English proverb, "Bread is the staff of life," is even more true when applied to Jesus. Jesus's flesh and life are offered to save us. He is the staff that gives us life. In Him, we will never die.

When Israel needed food in the wilderness, God miraculously provided manna from heaven. Moses was commanded to stack twelve loaves of bread on a table in the tabernacle as a reminder that God provides graciously for our needs.[70]

When thousands who follow Jesus are hungry, He miraculously fed them with "five barley loaves and two small fishes."[71] God generously provided bread to feed the body, but we need a different type of bread to receive everlasting life.

Jesus proclaimed, "I am the living bread which came down from heaven: if any man eat of this bread, he shall live forever: and the bread that I give is my flesh, which I will give for the life of the world."[72]

Many didn't comprehend Jesus's message of living bread. They were so focused on the bread that feeds the body that they failed to receive the Bread that feeds the soul. When the people asked Jesus for a miracle of more bread, He answered, "I am the bread of life: he that cometh to me shall never hunger; and he that believeth on me shall never thirst . . . This is the only work God wants from you: Believe in the one he has sent . . . He that believeth on me hath everlasting life."[73]

However, the people continued to focus on temporary bread. They "murmured at [Jesus], because he said, I am the bread which came down from heaven. And they said, Is not this Jesus, the son of Joseph, whose father and mother we know? how is it then that he saith, I came down from heaven?"[74]

Many failed to recognize Jesus as the Bread of Life and turn away from Him and follow Him no more.[75]

Without a sign of manna from the sky, they wouldn't believe. They wanted Jesus to give them bread to satisfy their physical hunger, but Jesus offered them something greater, saying, "No one who comes to me will ever be hungry, and no one who believes in me will ever be thirsty again."[76] Jesus is the manna from heaven who satisfies our hunger and the living water who quenches our thirst.

Everyone who ate manna in the wilderness eventually died,[77] but those who eat the "bread of life"[78] receive eternal life.

Whom Say Ye that I Am?

Jesus's name is the Bread of Life. Your new name is **filled**. "God, the source of hope, will fill you completely with joy and peace because you trust in him."[79] With Jesus, you "will never go hungry."[80]

Bridegroom

As the bridegroom rejoiceth over the bride, so shall thy God rejoice over thee.
Isaiah 62:5, King James Version

Being in a close relationship with another person can be very intimidating. We can be afraid of being rejected or that they won't have the same feelings toward us. However, there is one person who will never reject us, and is crazy about us. His name is Jesus Christ, our bridegroom.

A bridegroom is a man about to be married. Jesus has asked for our hand in marriage. He has asked us to take His name. He wants us as we are. He doesn't make us earn His proposal. He is already on one knee asking, "Will you marry me?" He has already accepted us as we are, but will we accept His proposal? Will we say yes, or will we deny His offer because we don't think we are worthy or good enough?

Many think we must earn Jesus's proposal. They are so busy trying to convince Jesus they are good enough they don't see Jesus down on one knee asking, "Will you marry me?" He has already proposed. We just have to accept.

He atoned in Gethsemane and died on the cross so He could be with us. He wants us to accept His proposal. Say yes to Jesus. Let Him put His ring on your finger and rejoice that Jesus loves you and wants to marry you. Accept all the amazing gifts He so desperately wants to give to you.

In the story of the ten virgins, there are five wise virgins who have oil, and five foolish virgins who don't have oil. The five who are wise find the bridegroom and join Him while the foolish virgins are locked out of the wedding. At the locked door, they cry saying, "Lord, Lord, open to us."[81] Then the bridegroom responds, "You know me not."[82] The foolish virgins didn't know the Savior and didn't have a relationship with Him. Meeting the bridegroom isn't about being righteous or being good enough to enter. It's about having a relationship with the bridegroom and wanting to be with Him.

When you marry the Savior, you inherit all He has. He is perfect so you inherit His perfection. You become perfect in Christ. Without Jesus, you are a sinner. With Him, you are perfect. Without Jesus, you are in debt. With Him, you are debt free.

The way to enter eternal life isn't a checklist of ordinances and things to do. It's a relationship with Jesus. We aren't trying to bring people to the church. We are trying to bring people to their Bridegroom to get married.

In a marriage covenant, the woman takes the groom's last name. Likewise, when we are baptized, we take the name of Christ. My new name is Mitchell Taylor Christ. Accept Jesus's marriage proposal. Take His name upon you. Accept His ring of justification and receive His gift of salvation.

In Stephen Robinson's book, *Believing Christ*, he compares our union with Christ to a marriage. He states,

> As husband and wife become one with each other through the covenant of marriage, so the Savior and the saved become one with each other through the covenant of the gospel. Just as a bride renounces all competing claims upon her loyalties and normally takes her husband's name, so those who enter this covenant with Christ renounce all competing loyalties, put Him first, and take His name upon them. To this union, we bring our righteous desires and our loyalty. He brings His perfection. In the covenant union, what is mine becomes His, and what is His becomes mine. Thus, my sins become His for payment, and His righteousness becomes mine for justification. When we become one with Jesus Christ, spiritually we form a partnership with a joint account, and His assets and our liabilities flow into each other. Since He has more assets than we have liabilities, the new account has a positive balance as soon as it is formed, and the partnership is justified, even though its junior partners (you and me) could not make it on their own. This is what the Apostle Paul refers to as being 'in Christ' (Colossians 1:28) and what Moroni calls being 'perfect in Christ' (Moroni 10:32).[83]

Jesus's name is Bridegroom. Your new name is **good enough**. When you enter a covenant with Jesus, He clothes you in His "robes of righteousness."[84]

Whom Say Ye that I Am?

Bright and Morning Star

I am the . . . bright and morning star.
Revelation 22:16, King James Version

We all are very familiar with the nativity story and a new star appearing in the heavens to testify that our Savior was born. Samuel the Lamanite declared, "And behold, there shall a new star arise, such an one as ye never have beheld."[85]

During New Testament times, people used the stars to guide them to their destination. Stars were the GPS of the day. This new star was given to guide people to Jesus—the Bright and Morning Star.

Whenever we feel lost, Jesus is the star that will guide us to safety. His light never ceases to shine. He is "a lamp to [our] feet and a light to [our] path."[86] Because Jesus is the Bright and Morning Star, we will "never walk in the darkness, but will have the light of life."[87]

Modern astrologers have called the planet Venus the morning star. It is the brightest star before the sun rises. Venus's shining light is a sign that a new day approaches.

Some days we will feel dark, lost, and hopeless, but every dark night is followed by a bright morning. In the darkness of night, we may feel the sun is gone, but the sun continues to shine just as brightly at midnight as at noon day. It is just blocked by the earth. When we feel like Christ's light is gone, you can know it is just blocked. Christ is our constant light that will never go out. He will never fail or leave us. Jesus is our shining light even when we are in darkness.

Jesus testifies that He is, "the light of the world."[88] His light shines to give us hope and dispense darkness. He is the Bright and Morning Star that lights our path and warms our souls.

Jesus's name is Bright and Morning Star. Your new name is **guided**. With Jesus, you will not lose your way for He is "the way."[89]

Mitchell C. Taylor

Captain of Salvation

For it became him, for whom are all things, and by whom are all things, in bringing many sons unto glory, to make the captain of their salvation perfect through sufferings.
Hebrews 2:10, King James Version

When I hear the word 'captain', I initially think of the movie *Captain Phillips* featuring Tom Hanks, which is based on a true story. Captain Phillips' ship was overtaken by pirates, and he was nearly killed. The pirates stormed the ship with machine guns and worked to take control of the ship. The leader of the pirates found Captain Phillips and commanded him at gunpoint, saying, "Look at me. Look at me!" Captain Phillips locked eyes with the leader of the pirates, who declared, "I am the captain now."

When someone is a captain, they are in control. The captain navigates the ship to its destination. We are each a ship driven on the sea of life in need of a captain to guide us safely to shore. Who will be the captain of your ship? Will you be like the pirate and say to Jesus, "I am the captain now," or will you let Jesus lead from the helm?

If we try to be the captain, we will be tossed to and fro by the winds of life. If we trust Jesus to be our captain, He will take us safely to the shores of the celestial kingdom. Even as the storms surge, the winds howl, and the waves crash into our boats, we can be calm and peaceful if Jesus is our captain.

Jesus is described as being "mighty to save."[90] Jesus's job is to save people. He isn't just good at saving people. He is perfect at saving people. He will save all who are on His ship.

There is no question as to whether Jesus's ship will arrive at the destination of eternal life and exaltation. His boat is headed full steam ahead and is guaranteed to arrive at the celestial kingdom. The real question is, will *you* be on His boat? Captain Jesus will sail His ship and all who are aboard safely back to a heavenly shore.

While Jesus was with His apostles on a boat, a great storm overtook them. The apostles feared they were going to die. In desperation, the apostles went to Jesus, who was sound asleep, and cried, "Master, carest thou not that we perish?"[91] Jesus arose and commanded the winds and the waves saying, "Peace! Be still!"[92] "And the wind ceased, and there was a great calm."[93] The apostles were astonished and "said one to another, What manner of man is this, that even the wind and the sea obey him?"[94] After Jesus rebuked the storm, He asked His apostles, "Why are ye so fearful? How is it that ye have no faith?"[95]

We all are like these apostles sometimes—fearful that the trials and challenges of life will drown us, and we initially try to save ourselves. The apostles were lowering the sail, holding firm to the rudder, and doing everything they could to save the boat. It wasn't until they turned to the Savior that they were saved.

Like these apostles, do we try to do everything possible before we turn to the Savior out of desperation? We should seek the Lord out of faith, not out of fear. We should go to the Lord first, knowing He can and will save us.

Jesus's name is Captain of Salvation. Your new name is **directed**. If Jesus is the captain of your life, He will "tell you all things what ye should do."[96] If Jesus is in your boat, it will not sink. Let Jesus be your Captain. Place your faith and trust in Him, and you will have no need for fear.

Carpenter

Is not this the carpenter's son?
Matthew 13:55, King James Version

When I was younger, it was hard for people to believe I was writing a book at such a young age. What they didn't see was that no matter how old I am I am a disciple of Jesus Christ with a God-given mission and ministry to write.

As Jesus shared the good news in synagogues, the people were astonished at His teaching and talked among themselves saying, "What is this wisdom He has been given? And how can He perform such miracles?"[97] Seeing Jesus teach so boldly and perform such mighty miracles, they complained, "Is not this the carpenter, the son of Mary?"[98]

The people in Jesus's day only saw Jesus as a carpenter. They couldn't wrap their minds around the idea that a carpenter could teach and perform miracles. They were so focused on Jesus being a carpenter that they couldn't see Jesus for who He truly was.

Is Jesus a carpenter from Nazareth or the promised Messiah? Is Jesus the son of Joseph and Mary, or is He the Son of God? The answer is He is all of these things. Yes, Jesus is a carpenter, but He is also the Messiah—the Savior and Redeemer of the world. Yes, Jesus is the son of Joseph and Mary, but He is also the Son of God.

Those who know Jesus only as the carpenter, son of Joseph and Mary, don't really know Him. Jesus does much more than fix broken tables. He mends broken hearts.

Do you know Jesus as the healer of your wounds? Do you know Jesus as your Savior and Redeemer? Do you know Jesus as the forgiver of your sins? Do you know Jesus as your best friend?

Only one person can save, redeem, heal, and forgive you, and that is Jesus of Nazareth, the Master Carpenter. We can't fix or cleanse ourselves. Jesus takes us from broken and blemished to a holy masterpiece.

Jesus's name is Carpenter. Your new name is **whole**. Jesus transforms you from broken to beautiful—from "wretched, pitiful, poor, blind and naked,"[99] to worthy, joyful, strong, and righteousness. Jesus is the Master Carpenter.

Chief Cornerstone

You, too, are built upon the foundation laid by the apostles and prophets the cornerstone being Jesus Christ.
Ephesians 2:20, Good News Translation

"A cornerstone is traditionally the first stone laid for a structure, with all other stones laid in reference. A cornerstone marks the geographical location by orienting a building in a specific direction."[100]

When we build our faith, Jesus should be the first stone laid to ensure a strong foundation and a correct orientation. We need Him to be the one the whole structure rests on. When Jesus is the chief corner stone of our faith, we won't be shaken. When earthquakes come, we won't be moved because we are founded upon "the rock of our Redeemer."[101]

The apostle Peter taught in Acts 4:11 that we are the builders of our faith. We choose what we learn and what we build our foundation on.

Nobody can force us to do anything. Will we be like the wise man, building a house upon the rock of Jesus, or like the foolish man, constructing a house on sand?

If we build our faith upon anything other than Christ, our foundation will eventually fail, and our faith will shatter. The Pharisees placed the law as the chief cornerstone of their faith. Each stone added had the law instead of Jesus as its guide for orientation and direction. As they built their faith stone by stone, they grew further and further from Jesus. When Jesus appeared, the Pharisees did not see Him as their chief cornerstone but as "a stone of stumbling."[102] The Pharisees rejected their Messiah because they had built their faith upon the cornerstone of the law.

Jesus should be the chief cornerstone of our faith. If Jesus isn't our base, the whole structure will collapse. On the other hand, when Jesus is our foundation, even when all manner of false doctrines and satanic counterfeits surround us, we will not fall because we are built on a sure foundation.

Jesus's name is Chief Cornerstone. Your new name is **immovable**. When you build on Jesus, you have a perfect foundation that will not fail.[103] "He who believes in [Jesus] will not be disappointed . . . and cannot fall."[104]

Christ, Messiah

And he shall be called Jesus Christ.
Mosiah 3:8

When we are born, we are given a name by our parents. Mary was told by an angel that she would "conceive and give birth to a son, and you will name him Jesus."[105]

Some tend to think Jesus Christ is Jesus's full name. With Jesus as his first name and Christ as His last name, but Mary wasn't told to name her baby Jesus Christ. She was told to name Him Jesus. Christ is a title that means deliverance, poetically and spiritually. The title "Christ" appears more than eleven hundred times in the scriptures. Jesus is *the* Christ.

The title "Christ" comes from the word *Christos*, which means "Anointed One." In the Old Testament, kings were anointed to show they had been chosen by God to serve His people. David was anointed by the prophet Samuel to be the King of Israel. Likewise, Jesus was anointed by His Father to come and save us from our fallen state. He was foreordained to be the Christ to save us all.[106]

The Jews anxiously watched for the prophesied Christ to be born and save them from their bondage to the Romans. Once Jesus began His earthly ministry, many people realized that He as the Christ prophesied of in the Old Testament. However, many others failed to recognize Jesus as the Christ and continue to wait for the Christ to come.

Jews during the ministry of Jesus believed the Christ would come to deliver them from the Romans. They desperately wanted to be freed from their Roman captors, but Jesus came to do more than relieve them from physical bondage. He came to free them from their bondage to sin and death.

While the apostles were with Jesus, He asked them a question, "Whom do men say that I the Son of Man am?"[107] His apostles replied, "some say that thou art John the Baptist: some, Elias; and others Jeremias, or one of the prophets."[108] Jesus then asked, "But whom say ye that I am?"[109] Peter answered, "Thou are the Christ, the Son of the living God."[110] Peter understood who Jesus was. He knew He was the Christ and His best friend. Do you know Jesus as the Christ and your best friend?

In the Book of Mormon, we read, "Wherefore, the prophets, and the priests, and the teachers, did labor diligently . . . persuading them to look forward unto the Messiah and believe in Him to come as though he already was."[111]

Not only did the prophets testify of Jesus's coming, but they told the people to believe in Jesus as though He already had come. Jesus is our Messiah, the anointed one, to deliver us from sin and death. We can choose whether to accept Him as the Messiah, or we can reject Him like the Pharisees. My prayer is that you will recognize Jesus as the Christ, the foreordained Messiah who came to save us all.

Jesus's name is Christ. Your new name is **set apart**. Jesus has called you by name and made you His.[112] He has set you apart from the world for His kingdom is not of this world.[113] He has prepared a mansion for you in the kingdom of heaven. "Be of good cheer . . . The kingdom is yours and the blessings thereof are yours, and the riches of eternity are yours."[114]

Whom Say Ye that I Am?

Commander, Leader

*Behold I have given him for a witness to the people,
a leader and commander to the people.*
Isaiah 55:4, King James Version

Throughout history, we have seen many remarkable leaders and commanders such as George Washington, Winston Churchill, Mahatma Gandhi, and Rosa Parks. These influential leaders were able to lead others and accomplish the impossible. Wouldn't it be awesome to have a leader like these people in our lives. We can have the greatest leader in the universe by our side every day—our Commander Jesus Christ.

When someone is a commander, they are delegated power from the group to help lead them to victory. This task is never easy, but when Jesus is on our side, we have no need to fear. He has all power, and whatever He commands is done.

Jesus is the greatest leader in all of history, but some decide not to listen to His commands. During His ministry, a Roman centurion came to Jesus and asked if He would heal his dying servant. When Jesus heard this, He responded, "I will come and heal him."[115]

The centurion, bowing on one knee, replied, "Lord, I am not worthy that thou shouldest come under my roof: but speak the word only, and my servant shall be healed. For I am a man of authority, having soldiers under me: and I say to this man, Go, and he goeth; and to another, Come, and he cometh; and my servant, Do this, and he doeth it."[116]

Jesus then told the centurion, "Go thy way; and as thou hast believed, so be it done unto thee. And his servant was healed the selfsame hour."[117]

This centurion understood Jesus's power and knew that whatsoever He commanded is done. This centurion, a man of great power and authority, recognized that Jesus had far greater power than him. He humbled himself before the true Commander and pleaded for Him to heal his servant.

Is Jesus the Commander of our lives? Who makes the decisions? Who leads and guides us? Sometimes we may think we have earthly power like a centurion, but once we experience the love and power of Jesus, we exclaim like Moses, "Now . . . I know that man is nothing."[118]

We see who has all power and who is in control. We need to let Jesus take full control of our lives. We need to follow His commands. We need to be like Jesus's mother at the wedding in Cana and exclaim, "Whatever He may say to [me], [I will] do it."[119]

All other commanders and leaders will eventually fail or lose a battle, but not Jesus. He has never lost a battle. While the battles between good and evil, light and dark, and Jesus and Satan rage on, there is no questions about who will win. We know Jesus will win the war.

The battle is not to see who will win because that outcome has already been determined. The battle is to determine which side you, your family, and your friends will be on. We are not fighting to determine who will win the war. We are fighting to ensure our family and friends are on the winning side.

With Jesus as your Leader and Commander, you are guaranteed victory. "The LORD your God is with you. He is a hero who saves you. He happily rejoices over you, renews you with his love, and celebrates over you with shouts of joy."[120] Jesus gives you this promise, "I will give you victory."[121]

Jesus has won the battle over sin and death. Jesus is the perfect Commander who doesn't lose. We have no need to fear, because, we "know in whom [we] have trusted."[122]

Jesus's name is Commander. Your new name is **victorious.** Jesus "fought the good fight."[123] He exclaimed from the cross, "It is finished!"[124] Through your Lord and Commander, Jesus Christ "death is destroyed; victory is complete!"[125]

Confidence

Thou art my Confidence.
Job 31:24, King James Version

In our world today, we are constantly bombarded with things we can do to become a better person. We are told to build self-confidence and trust in our abilities. We are told to not hurt others' self-esteem. We are told to be self-reliant and to not depend on others. Millions of self-help books are published each year, yet people are still depressed, unfulfilled, and discouraged. What is the solution?

We emphasize self—self-confidence, self-esteem, self-reliance, and self-help—when we should emphasize Christ. Instead of telling people to build self-confidence, we should teach them about to build Christ-confidence. Instead of self-esteem, we need Christ-esteem. Instead of self-reliance, we need Christ-reliance. Trusting in ourselves is not the answer. Philippians 3:3 teaches to "rely on what Christ Jesus has done for us . . . put no confidence in human effort."[126] Jesus is the true source of "confidence for everyone."[127]

When we are anxious or worried, it is evidence that we are trusting in ourselves instead of having confidence in Christ. Rick Warren has taught, "Worry is really just a form of atheism. Every time you worry, you're acting like an atheist. You're saying, 'It all depends on me.' That's just not in the Bible."

The Hebrew word for confidence, *bitachon*, means to be open. This suggests that nothing is hidden from view, that you see the whole picture. When we put our trust in ourselves, we worry because we are finite in our abilities and constantly make mistakes. When we trust in Jesus, we don't have to worry because Jesus is infinite and perfect.

There is only one way to be saved, and it's through Jesus Christ. "The world teaches us to be self-sufficient, self-reliant, self-motivating. But anytime we put self before Savior, we're in trouble. We must be reliant on *Him* in order to stand strong and tall and brave."[128] True confidence doesn't come from self. It comes from Jesus.

We must "remain in Christ, so that when He appears, we may be confident and unashamed before Him."[129] If we want to be confident before God, we must be in a relationship with Jesus. Jesus is the only way to enter the Kingdom of God. If you want to return to live with God, "do not throw away your confidence, which has a great reward."[130] Don't let go of your confidence in Christ because once you take Jesus out of the picture, you will begin to crumble and fall.

We all will have doubts and fears. It's in our nature. We are human and are limited in our abilities and our understanding. But we are loved by an unlimited, all-knowing God who cannot fail. We don't have to cross our fingers and hope we are good enough. We can have confidence we are saved by Jesus because He is good enough.

Jesus's name is Confidence. Your new name is **confident**. When you understand your relationship with Jesus, you can declare, "I am confident that God will save me."[131]

Counselor

. . . and his name will be called . . . Counselor.
Isaiah 9:6, New King James Version

I love basketball and have played it since I was very young. When I was younger, I wanted to play on a school basketball team, so I went to my church gym every day and practiced. I was homeschooled, but I didn't let that get in my way. However, the fact that I was homeschooled did change how I was seen by the coaches. I made the team my eighth grade and freshman year but didn't get much playing time. I was equally good or better than some of the players who got more playing time, but I sat bench.

After my freshman year, I was sick of being a bench warmer, so I increased my training and worked extremely hard. I got to the point where I was shooting sixty percent from three and eighty percent inside. I had a laser of a shot. As tryouts neared, I was ecstatic. The coach for the junior varsity team loved shooting three pointers, and I thought this was my chance to prove I was good, even though I was homeschooled.

Tryouts started and I played extremely well. The other players didn't pass to me a lot, but when they did, you could count on my shot going in. I survived the first couple cuts of tryouts, but on the fourth day at the end of tryouts, coach pulled me to the side and told me, "Mitchell, you're a great player, but you didn't make the team. I want you to prove me wrong. Prove that I made the wrong decision."

As soon as I heard him say this, I was distraught. I held in all my emotions, grabbed my stuff, and drove home. Once I got home, I fell on my bed and cried for an hour. I thought this year was my chance to prove I could play ball, but all my hard work was wasted.

Whom Say Ye that I Am?

My sadness began to turn into rage, and I took my coach's words to heart. I was going to prove him wrong. As the days went by, my mom asked me, "Why do you want to play basketball?"

I answered, "Because I love the game."

She then asked, "Is it worth it if you never play? Could the time you use to practice be used for something else?"

Her words changed my perspective, and I started focusing on other things. She helped me make the decision to move forward.

Like my mom, some people in our lives guide us when we feel lost, comfort us when we feel alone, and strengthen us when we feel weak. Alongside all our wonderful friends, we also have a perfect counselor in Jesus Christ. He is by our side, guiding, comforting and assisting us.

When Jesus is called Counselor, it is translated from the word *ya'ats*, which means, to advise, resolve, and counsel. When we feel like we have nowhere to turn for peace or guidance, we can always turn to Jesus. He awaits our call for help. He will always do what is best for us. He desires that we find true joy.

Alma 37:37 declares, "Counsel with the Lord in all thy doings, and he will direct thee for good." We are commanded to counsel with God in all things, whether physical, financial, or spiritual. The Lord wants to help us.

We all have a natural tendency to not want assistance. We want to try and do everything on our own. We know we need help, but we are afraid to ask for it. Whenever you feel afraid to ask for help, you can know Satan is trying to keep you away from the loving hand of Christ. Satan makes us think that we are weak. Satan wants us to be ashamed when we ask for assistance. Seeking Jesus for help is a strength not a weakness—an act of faith and power.

Asking for help isn't bad. We all need it. Especially when it comes to our salvation and exaltation. We all need the Lord's guiding counsel in our lives. He is the one true counselor who will never tire of helping a sick sinner like us. He absolutely adores each one of us.

Another tactic of Satan's is to make you believe you aren't worthy of Jesus's assistance. He doesn't want you to come to Jesus, because he knows what will happen to you if you enter the embrace of Jesus Christ.

Jesus doesn't care about what you have done. He wants to help you become like Him. Jacob 4:10, states, "Wherefore, seek not to counsel the

Lord, but to take counsel from his hand." Jesus's advice and counsel is the perfect source to look to. He is our loving and compassionate Counselor.

Jesus's name is Counselor. Your new name is **comforted**. Jesus gives you this promise: "I will not leave you comfortless: I will come to you."[132]

Creator

For by him were all things created.
Colossians 1:16, King James Version

We all have created wonderful things that bring a smile to our face. We are God's creations, and seeing us learn and grow brings a huge smile to His face. Nothing makes God happier than seeing His children happy.

Our Lord and Savior is the creator of everything. "All things were made by him and without him was not anything made that was made."[133] Jesus is "the Father of heaven and earth, the Creator of all things from the beginning."[134]

As our Creator, Jesus knows our potential. We are created in the image of God the Father and Jesus Christ.[135] Their work and glory is to bring to pass the immortality and eternal life of man.[136] We were created to eventually become like Them.

Some think they don't need our Creator. They think they know better how to achieve happiness and fulfillment. However, Jesus knows us better than we know ourselves. He created us and knows perfectly how we work. We need to look to Him for instruction because He owns the manual on how to become our best selves.

Many competing ideas and voices try to tell us how to live, but we will not answer to a professor, psychologist, scientist, economist, or doctor in the next life. We will answer to the Lord Jesus. Since we will answer to Him there, we should listen to Him here.[137]

There is no better person to trust than the Creator Himself. He loves us intensely and was willing to die for each one of us. We can't do anything without our Creator because without Him, "[we] can do nothing."[138] He saved us from physical and spiritual death and gave us a body so we could become like Him.

Whom Say Ye that I Am?

Jesus is our Creator. We didn't magically create ourselves, and we cannot magically save ourselves. Both tasks require our Creator, Jesus Christ.

Jesus's name is Creator. Your new name is **son or daughter of God**. You are His child. He will do anything to help you have joy and happiness. Men and women "are, that they might have joy."[139] God smiles when He sees you happy.

Deliverer

The LORD is my rock, my fortress and my deliverer; my God is my rock, in whom I take refuge, my shield and the horn of my salvation, my stronghold.
Psalm 18:2, New International Version

I love to watch basketball, especially the Utah Jazz. One of my favorite basketball players of all time is Karl Malone. One of Karl Malone's famous nicknames is "The Mailman"—because he always delivers. He wasn't afraid of anyone between him and the basket. Karl Malone delivered a lot of points and powerful dunks.

While Karl Malone delivered for the Utah Jazz, Jesus delivers for you and me. Just as Karl Malone didn't let anything stop him from getting to the rim, Jesus doesn't let anything stop Him from saving us.

Jesus is a mighty deliverer. He delivers us from a variety of difficulties and dangers. Whatever it may be, you can count on Jesus to deliver.

He delivered the children of Israel from the bondage of Egypt.
He delivered Esther and her people from being massacred.
He delivered His disciples from a raging storm on the Sea of Galilee.
He delivered Gideon from the hands of his enemies.
He delivered David from Goliath.
He delivered you and me from sin and gives us His kingdom.
Jesus has promised, "In distress you called, and I delivered you;"[140]

Jesus didn't come to give eloquent speeches. Jesus came to deliver. Nothing is too hard for our God. Jesus has come, "to save."[141]

There is only one deliverer, and it isn't you or me. It's Jesus. We can't save ourselves or do any part of the saving. No matter how hard we try, we can't deliver ourselves from the chains of sin. Only Christ has the key to unlock the bondage of sin and deliver us from our captor. Jesus sets us free.

Jesus's name is Deliverer. Your new name is **delivered**. "Everyone who calls on the name of the Lord will be delivered."[142]

Door

I am the door of the sheep.[143]
—Jesus (John 10:7 King James Version)

In the Book of Mormon, Lehi shares his vision of the tree of life. In this dream, Lehi "saw numberless concourses of people, many of whom were pressing forward, that they might obtain the path which led unto the tree."[144] The people were trying to find the way to the tree, but many "wandered off and were lost."[145] The ones who made it were those who held fast to the rod and fell down at the tree.[146] There is only one way to the tree of life—Jesus.

During Christ's ministry, He constantly taught the Pharisees that they were sinners and that the only way to be saved was through the Savior. However, the Pharisees believed that they had found a way to be saved by obedience to the law. In John chapter 10, Jesus teaches, "I am the door of the sheep . . . and he that entereth not by the door . . . is a thief and a robber."[147] Anyone who says there is a way other than Jesus is a false shepherd.

Some will say they have discovered another way to be saved, but you can know they are lying because, "Salvation exists in no one else, for there is no other name under heaven given to men by which we must be saved."[148] Salvation is only through the door of Jesus Christ. "Salvation belongs to the Lord."[149]

When you know Jesus is the only way to be saved, "[You] will never follow a stranger, but will run away from him because [you] do not recognize the stranger's voice."[150]

There is only one way into the sheepfold, and that way is Jesus. He is the door we need to enter through. There is only one way to be saved, and it's through the "name of Christ, the Lord Omnipotent."[151]

Whom Say Ye that I Am?

Jesus's name is Door. Your new name is **abundant**. All who join the fold of Christ are given an abundant life. Jesus declares, "I am come that they might have life, and that they might have it more abundantly."[152]

El Shaddai

God appeared to [Abram], and said to him, 'I am El Shaddai. Walk before me, and be blameless.'
Genesis 17:1, New Heart English Bible

The Hebrew words *El Shaddai* found in the Old Testament are often translated as God Almighty or Almighty God. This translation doesn't fully capture the meaning of *El Shaddai*. *Shaddai* is the Hebrew word meaning two danglers or teat.

"The goat was a very common animal within the herds of the Hebrews. It produces milk within the udder and is extracted by the goat kid by squeezing and sucking on the two teats dangling below the udder. The function of these teats is to provide all the necessary nourishment for the kids, as they would die without it. The Hebrew word ידש (shaddai) also has the meaning of a 'teat.' Just as the goat provides nourishment to its kids through the milk, God nourishes His children through His milk and provides all the necessities of life."[153]

A more accurate translation of the Hebrew words *El Shaddai* would be "The Mighty Teat." "Many times a translator will not translate a Hebrew word literally because the literal meaning would mean nothing to the Western mind and in some cases would actually be offensive to the Western reader. Such is the case with the word ידש (*shaddai*). The use of the word 'Almighty' by the translator is his attempt at translating the text in a manner that will both make sense to the Western reader as well as retain some of the meaning of the original Hebrew word."[154]

The symbolism of Jesus referring to Himself as *El Shaddai* is powerful and instructive. The Hebrew word for mother is *em*, which means strong glue. The word *em* is used for mother because she binds the family together. She holds tightly and securely to her children to care for and protect them. The idea of Jesus as our mother is a powerful symbol that He is the mighty glue that holds us tightly and securely to Him to nourish and protect us.

The imagery of a nursing mother also provides powerful symbolism. When a baby is born, she relies solely on her mother for nourishment. Likewise, Jesus is our only source of nourishment. If a mother were to stop nursing her baby, the baby would die. The baby's only food is the mother's milk. Likewise, Jesus nourishes and strengthens us. Without Him, we die. He is our only source of nourishment.

Sometimes we may feel that we can rely on our own actions or resources to provide for ourselves, but we should remember that we are all babies completely dependent on Jesus. We can't save ourselves or provide for ourselves. We need to recognize our complete dependence on Jesus, or we will never be in the right relationship with Him.

Jesus, our *El Shaddai*, will not only will give us nourishment, but He will also give us everything we need. Jesus has promised, "I have come to give you everything in abundance, more than you expect—life in its fullness until you overflow!"[155]

Jesus's name is *El Shaddai*. Your new name is **nourished**. Jesus gives you this promise, "I will nourish you . . . and [I] will give you everything you need."[156] Jesus is your *El Shaddai*.

El Simkhat Gili

There I will go to the altar of God . . . the source of all my joy.
Psalm 43:4, New Living Translation

We all want happiness and joy, but sometimes happiness feels impossible. We are told in 2 Nephi 2:25 that "men [and women] are, that they might have joy." If God created us to have joy, why do we still feel lonely and depressed? At times, we may cry like Jesus from the cross, "My God, my God, why have you abandoned me?"[157] We have been taught that Jesus lives and loves us, but sometimes we don't feel it. How can we find joy in Jesus, even when we feel lost, sad, and alone?

Psalm 43 expresses how we sometimes feel; "God . . . why have you tossed me aside? Why must I wander around in grief . . . Why am I discouraged? Why is my heart so sad?"[158]

Whom Say Ye that I Am?

This psalmist responded to their grief, pain, and depression by saying, "God, my only safe haven . . . send out your light and your truth; let them guide me. Let them lead me to . . . you—the source of all my joy. I will praise you . . . O God, my God! I will put my hope in God! I will praise him again—my Savior and my God!"[159]

Russell M. Nelson taught, ". . . the joy we feel has little to do with the circumstances of our lives and everything to do with the focus of our lives."[160] If we want to find true joy, we should do as the psalmist and plead for God's light, truth, and joy. We should praise Jesus again and again. If you want to be filled from the fountains of Jesus's joy, repeat out loud Psalm 43 again and again:

"God, my only safe haven . . . send out your light and your truth; let them guide me. Let them lead me to . . . you—the source of all my joy. I will praise you . . . O God, my God! I will put my hope in God! I will praise him again—my Savior and my God!"[161]

Life is full of darkness, challenges, grief, and pain. You can search the Bible, the Book of Mormon and Doctrine and Covenants, and you will not find a promise of a pain-free life, but you will find the repeated words of the Savior, "Be of good cheer."[162]

El Simkhat Gili is a Hebrew phrase that means "God my exceeding joy" or "God my joyful joy." Jesus is no ordinary joy. He is a joy that exceeds all understanding. He is the joy of joys. Jesus doesn't want us just thinking about Him. He wants us to experience Him. He wants us to enjoy Him. He is our friend and wants us to be happy. He wants us to drink from His fountain of uncontainable joy. Our relationship with Jesus can fill us with joy even in the most adverse circumstances imaginable.

Some try to hide, dull, or escape their pain, grief, or depression with drugs, sex, or video games, but these will not bring joy. By connecting with *El Simkhat Gili*—the source of all joy—we can be of good cheer even through our pain, grief, and sadness. In our darkest hours, will we turn to God or will we turn to the world. "May God, the fountain of hope, fill you to overflowing with uncontainable joy and perfect peace as you trust in him."[163]

Jesus's name is *El Simkhat Gilit*. Your new name is **delighted**. Jesus promises you joy, peace, and delight, "I will give [you] joy."[164] "[I] will give you peace . . . [I] will bring delight to your soul."[165] Jesus is your exceeding joy. If you look to Him and praise His name, you can be joyful no matter your circumstances, and declare, "My soul [is] joyful in the Lord."[166]

The Everlasting Father

His name shall be called . . . The everlasting Father
Isaiah 9:6, King James Version

While my mom was at an orphanage in Ecuador, a baby began to cry. My mom, being a loving mother, went to pick up the crying baby. My mom was told she could not pick up the baby. The staff member said, "If we allowed visitors to hold the babies, the babies would want to be held once the visitors were gone, and we don't have enough staff to do this." It hurts my soul to see children without a mom or dad to hold and comfort them.

Sadly, some babies never know how it feels to be held, loved, and comforted by a mother or father. Being a child is supposed to be fun with new discoveries and adventures each day. However, this is not the case for all children. While the relationship each person has with their birth mother and father will vary greatly from person to person, one family relationship can be the same for everyone.

We are children of a loving Heavenly Father, and when we enter into a covenant relationship with Christ, we take upon ourselves Christ's name and become part of Christ's family. Which is why both Heavenly Father and Jesus are, at times, referred to as Father.

Jesus wants us to be a part of His family. Jesus wants to hold, comfort, and love you. When we come to Jesus, He adopts us into His family and calls us His. He says, "Do not fear, for I have redeemed you; I have called you by name; you are Mine!"[167] You become His child and He becomes your Father. He is a perfect father who has promised to "never leave you or abandon you."[168] Jesus will be our Father forever and ever.

Jesus loves us so much that He gave His life for us. Doctrine and Covenants 18:10–11 teaches, "the worth of souls is great in the sight of God; For, behold, the Lord your Redeemer suffered death in the flesh; wherefore he suffered the pain of all men, that all men might repent and come unto him." As our Everlasting Father, He wants each one of us to be with Him. The Bible tells us that Jesus "will draw everyone to [Him]."[169]

Jesus isn't an ordinary dad. He is our chosen Father. Our covenant Father, Jesus Christ, wants what is best for us. He wants to bless, nourish, and teach us. He wants us to inherit all the Father hath.[170] We will receive everlasting life through our Everlasting Father. Jesus is always by our side to lead and guide us. He has promised, "I will not abandon you as orphans"[171]

Jesus's name is The Everlasting Father. Your new name is **haniai**. Haniai is a Hebrew word that means a place to rest and to be happy. Jesus's family is a place of peace, rest, and never-ending happiness. Jesus, your Everlasting Father, is with you always. You are a member of Jesus's family forever.

Exemplar

For God called you to do good, even if it means suffering, just as Christ suffered for you. He is your example, and you must follow in his steps.
1 Peter 2:21, New Living Translation

Our goal in life is to become like Jesus Christ. We are to serve and be kind like He was. We are to lose our lives in the service of others. We are to comfort and lift those around us. We are to go about doing good.[172] However, in our endeavor to follow Jesus, we will be nowhere near perfection. Only one lived perfectly, and that is Jesus Christ.

Some believe that in order to gain the celestial kingdom, you have to be perfect by your own efforts. Thankfully, this is not the case. Jesus came and died for us precisely because we aren't perfect. "God showed his great love for us by sending Christ to die for us while we were still sinners."[173]

Jesus died so we could learn and grow and still return to live with Him again. Our job isn't to be perfect and sinless. Jesus took care of sin in Gethsemane and on the cross. Our job is to "endure to the end, in following the example of the Son of the living God."[174] We are to strive every day to become more like Jesus. We move slowly on the path of sanctification to become more and more like Christ. We don't do this to prove ourselves worthy. We do this to learn, grow, and become.

Jesus's life is our example of how to live. We are to look to Him, "in every thought"[175] and "not depend on [our] own understanding."[176] If we will look to Christ and trust in His hand, He will "tell you all things what ye should do."[177] We should continually ask, "What would Jesus do?" and follow the prompting we receive. President Russell M. Nelson has given us this prophetic warning, "In coming days, it will not be possible to survive spiritually without the guiding, directing, comforting, and constant influence of the Holy Ghost."[178] Make Jesus your guide and example.

Jesus's name is Exemplar. Your new name is **exemplary**. When you are with Christ, "your light shine[s] before others . . . and give[s] glory to your Father who is in heaven."[179]

Firstborn

"I was in the beginning with the Father, and am the Firstborn.[180]
—Jesus (Doctrine and Covenants 93:21)

I grew up as the oldest living child in my home. At times, it was a difficult role to play, with siblings looking up to me and following my example, regardless of what I was doing. I often was crushed by the weight of my shortcomings and wondered why the Lord had made me the oldest sibling when I couldn't measure up.

While I am not a perfect older brother, we all have one who is—the Firstborn, Jesus Christ. Jesus is the perfect older brother we can look to for guidance. He is always loving and compassionate. He won't yell at you or argue with you. He is our perfect friend and brother.

In the movie *Aladdin*, the genie sings the song "Friend Like Me." The genie tells Aladdin all these amazing things he can do for him and finishes be repeating many times, "You ain't never had a friend like me." While the genie has some amazing powers, they are minuscule in comparison to Jesus. The truth is we ain't never had a friend like Jesus. He is the greatest friend we will ever have.

Mary was the earthly mother of Jesus, but Jesus had no earthly father of His flesh. God is the literal spiritual and physical Father of Jesus. Jesus is the Firstborn of the Father in spirit and the first and only begotten in the flesh. The word translated to "Only Begotten" from Greek is *monogenes,* which means one of a kind. Jesus is our unique, one-of-a-kind brother.

As a good big brother, Jesus protects us against bullies. Jesus is the only one who can protect us from the bullies of sin and death. Our big brother was willing to die to save us. The apostle John wrote of His friend and brother Jesus Christ, "Greater love has no one than this, that a person will lay down his life for his friends."[181]

The big bully, Lucifer, runs and hides when Jesus is around. Satan has no power when we stay close to Jesus. "Remember that it is upon the rock of our Redeemer, who is Christ, the Son of God, that ye must build your foundation; that when the devil shall send forth his mighty winds, yea, his shafts in the whirlwind, yea, when all his hail and his mighty storm shall beat upon you, it shall have no power over you to drag you down to the gulf of misery and endless wo."[182]

Jesus's name is Firstborn. Your new name is **defended**. Jesus is an awesome big brother who defends us against the bullies of sin, death, and Satan. "The Lord is your mighty defender, perfect and just in all his ways."[183]

Friend of Sinners

The Son of man is come eating and drinking; and ye say, Behold a gluttonous man, and a winebibber, a friend of publicans and sinners!
Luke 7:34, King James Version

We all want to have friends and be accepted by others. We are social creatures and desperately want others to like us. When I was five years old, I lived in Utah. I didn't have many friends, and the neighborhood we lived in didn't have any children my age. I did have one friend, Paul Monson, who was eight years older than me. He would come to my house and play on the trampoline and play video games. My much older friend meant the world to me. I never forced him to be my friend, he accepted me even though I was significantly younger than him. He chose me instead of being with friends his age, and we are still friends to this day. Thanks, Paul!

Jesus is our friend. He accepts us as we are and doesn't judge us by our past. He wants to be with us every single day. Jesus's title, Friend of Sinners, was used by the Pharisees to try and tear Him down. This so-called evil name turned out to be a beautiful name that testifies of truth.

Jesus has come to be with sinners. Jesus declared, "For the Son of Man has come to save the lost."[184] The Pharisees looked down on those who affiliated with those labeled as sinners, but this didn't bother Jesus. Jesus is a friend to all. He says, "Come unto me, all of you . . . and I shall give you rest."[185]

The Pharisees condemned Jesus for hanging out with sinners, even though they too were sinners. Jesus can only be friends with sinners because we are all sinners. Romans 3:10 declares, "There is no one who is righteous."[186]

Jesus declares, "For I have come [not to be friends to] those who think they are righteous, but those who know they are sinners."[187] Thinking we are righteous by our actions distances us from Jesus. Knowing we are sinners puts us in the correct state for a friendship with Jesus. The prophet Alma teaches that you should "acknowledge your unworthiness before God at all times."[188] The apostle John declares, "If we say that we have no sin, we deceive ourselves, and the truth is not in us."[189]

To follow the prophet Alma, the apostle John, and the Savior himself, we should acknowledge that we are unworthy sinners at all times. "There is none righteous, no, not one."[190] Yes, we are all unworthy sinners, but that's okay because Jesus is a friend of sinners.

One morning during our family *Come, Follow Me* study, we were reading in Matthew chapter 26: "Now when Jesus was in Bethany, in the house of Simon the leper, There came unto him a woman having an alabaster box of very precious ointment, and poured it on his head, as he sat at meat. But when his disciples saw it, they had indignation, saying, To what purpose is this waste? For this ointment might have been sold for much, and given to the poor. When Jesus understood it, he said unto them, Why trouble ye the woman? . . . Verily I say unto you, Wheresoever this gospel shall be preached in the whole world, there shall also this, that this woman hath done, be told for a memorial of her."[191]

Whom Say Ye that I Am?

This verse seemed to jump from the page, "Wheresoever this gospel shall be preached in the whole world, there shall also this, that this woman hath done, be told for a memorial of her." [192]

Why does Jesus direct that this story be shared whenever the gospel is preached? As we discussed this question as a family, my dad said, "I have been teaching the good news of Jesus Christ for twenty years, and I can't remember a time I have taught this story as a part of the good news."

My dad's comment struck me. I wanted to know why Jesus wanted this story to be remembered and taught throughout the world, so I began pondering and praying about these verses. As I pondered and studied, I began to wonder why, with the many powerful stories Jesus could have requested to be taught with the gospel, this story is the one Jesus requested be shared. This story is included with the events of Jesus's suffering in the Garden of Gethsemane, His crucifixion, and His resurrection. Why were these verses important enough to be included with such momentous events? There had to be a reason, but I wasn't seeing it yet.

A few days later, my dad and I were discussing what we had learned about this story from our individual study. We had learned that the events had taken place in the home of Simon, who had been healed of leprosy. We learned that Lazarus, whom Jesus raised from the dead, had also been in the house.

"Dad," I said. "Why do you think Jesus would request the story of a woman anointing Him with ointment be shared with the gospel and not the story of Simon being healed of leprosy or the story of Lazarus being raised from the dead? Those seem like more important stories to me."

As we talked about this question, the inspiration came. Jesus can heal your sickness, and He can raise you from the dead, but His greatest gift is forgiving your sins.

This woman was a sinner who was forgiven by Jesus. She received His grace. She was born again through Jesus's redeeming power. She heard the good news and was changed. She received Jesus's gifts of peace, love, forgiveness, and joy. She became friends with Jesus and put her faith and trust in Him.

Each time we hear the story of Jesus's victory over sin and death, Jesus wants us to hear this woman's story. Jesus wants to ensure that the gospel is not just information that is taught but a relationship that transforms. This woman's story invites us to be friends with Jesus.

Jesus wants each of us to receive His gifts of forgiveness, salvation, and friendship with the same joy and gratitude this woman does. She was so grateful to her Friend and Savior that she anointed Him with expensive ointment, an honor that was rare even for kings. Jesus rejoices when we are His friends.

Some criticized Jesus for sitting with sinners and allowing sinners to touch Him. Jesus wants the story of this woman to be told so we each know He wants us close to Him, and He sits with and embraces sinners.

Jesus's name is Friend of Sinners. Your new name is **my friend**. Jesus is your best friend. Jesus calls you by name and says, "You are my friend."[193] Jesus says to you, "We will share a meal together as friends."[194]

Gift

Wherefore, by faith was the law of Moses given. But in the gift of his Son hath God prepared a more excellent way; and it is by faith that it hath been fulfilled.
Ether 12:11

Christmas is one of my favorite times of year. We share gifts, sing Christmas carols, and drink hot chocolate, but most importantly we remember the birth of our Savior, Jesus Christ.

We all have gone to a Christmas party or mall to sit on Santa's lap and tell him what we want for Christmas. Santa usually asks, "Were you a good boy or girl this year?" Without hesitation we answer yes because we want to receive presents from Santa. On Christmas morning, we sprint to the Christmas tree to find our gifts.

When we receive gifts from Santa, we may think we earned the gifts because we were nice that year. Likewise, sometimes we think gifts from our Heavenly Father are earned by being nice. The dictionary describes a gift as "a thing given willingly to someone without payment." A gift is something that is not paid for. You can't earn or pay for a gift, or it is no longer a gift. On Christmas, do you give someone a gift because you feel they earned it? That thought has never crossed my mind. We give gifts to people because we love them.

Whom Say Ye that I Am?

God's gifts aren't conditioned on whether you are good enough. Heavenly Father gives us the gift of His perfect Son because He loves us. "For God so loved the world that he gave his only begotten son, that whosoever believeth in him should not perish but have everlasting life."[195]

Jesus loves us so much that He was willing "to give his life as a ransom for many."[196] He gave His life as a gift.

Heavenly Father and Jesus are the most generous gift givers in the universe. Heavenly Father and Jesus desperately want you to accept their gift of eternal life. Will you accept the gift? Or will you "neglect your gift?"[197]

"Gift" in Greek is the word *charis* which means grace. Grace (Jesus) is a gift from God. We can't earn eternal life or Jesus's love. There is nothing you can do for Jesus to love you more, and there is nothing you can do for Jesus to love you less. Jesus loves you unconditionally and wants to save you.

When you receive a gift on Christmas, someone had to buy the present. Someone paid the price for the gift, but that isn't the receiver's job. Would you take your Christmas gift to the store and try to pay for it again? Jesus paid the price for your gift of eternal life so you wouldn't have to. There is no way for you to pay for the gifts Christ gives you. Your job is to receive them.

The apostle Paul taught, "For the wages of sin is death, but the free gift of God is eternal life in union with the Messiah Jesus our Lord."[198]

You don't have to pay a single penny toward the gifts of grace and eternal life. Jesus has already paid for your gifts in full. There is no more debt, no fee. It is a gift.

Jesus's name is Gift. Your new name is **blessed**. Jesus laid down His life so you could have "His indescribable gift"[199] of eternal life!

God

Fear thou not; for I am with thee: be not dismayed; for I am thy God.
Isaiah 41:10, King James Version

We are all very familiar with the name "God." However, much of this name's beautiful meaning has been lost. The central truth running throughout Jewish scripture is this: there is one true God, and He is the only hope of our salvation.[200] Judaism uses many names to refer to the one and only Creator and Ruler of the universe: El, Elohim, Eloch, Elohai, El Shaddai, etc. These names are translated to God, the living God, the God of Hosts, the God Almighty, etc.

"God" is the English translation of the Hebrew words used to describe their God. Jesus is this God. He is the God of Israel. Heavenly Father sent His Son, Jesus Christ, that all mankind might be saved. Jesus is our hope of salvation.

In Isaiah chapter 44, Jesus asks and answers a question, "Is there any God besides me? No . . . I know not one."[201]

The second commandment God gave to Moses is this, "Thou shalt have no other gods before me."[202] Anything that seeks to replace Jesus is a false god.

We should ask these questions, "What or who do I allow to be my God? What or who do I allow to rule my life?" Video games, sports, church, good works, and family can all be gods. There are many false gods, but there is only one true and living God.

Jesus's name is God. Your new name is **known.** God knows you by name.[203] Jesus says to you as he did to Moses, "I know you."[204] Let Jesus be your advocate. Put your faith and trust in Him. Over two dozen times throughout the Bible, the Book of Mormon, Doctrine and Covenants, and Pearl of Great Price, Jesus declares, "I am God."[205]

Good Shepherd

I am the good shepherd, and the good shepherd gives up his life for his sheep.
John 10:11, Contemporary English Version

I absolutely love sheep. They are cute, fluffy, and resemble clouds. Even though they are fluffy white clouds of cuteness, they are also one of the dumbest animals on the planet. If the shepherd takes his eyes off the sheep for one minute, they will wander from the herd to fall off a cliff, be eaten by a wolf, or somehow manage to get injured.

Sheep need constant care, or they will die. We all are little sheep who need to be constantly looked after. We wander, get stuck, and injure ourselves. Without the aid of a shepherd, we would all perish. Thankfully, we have a Good Shepherd who is by our side 24/7/365. He stays by our side, no matter how many times we mess up. He will never kick us out of His fold.

In Hebrew, the word 'shepherd' comes from the word *ra'ah* which means friend. "The shepherd is not a distant ruler or overseer, but a constant companion and friend to the flock. He spends more time with his flock . . . then he does with his own family. Our relationship with God is meant to be this type of relationship, where we become intimate friends with our guardian, protector, and provider."[206]

We have the greatest Shepherd of all time. Jesus isn't a hired hand. When a hired hand "sees the wolf coming, he abandons the sheep and runs away."[207] Jesus is the Good Shepherd. He will destroy the wolves that try to destroy us. He will bind our wounds every time we fall. His love is so great that He is willing to lay down His life for us, His sheep.

While Jesus is the Good Shepard, there will be hired hands and thieves that only care to use you for their own personal gain. They worry more about themselves than the flock. Ezekiel 34:2 implores, "What sorrow awaits you shepherds who feed yourselves instead of your flocks. Shouldn't shepherds feed their sheep?"[208] We need to beware of these false shepherds. We need to follow our Good Shepherd who cares more about us than himself.

A plethora of voices strive to lead us another way. We need to have a relationship with our Shepherd so we will "follow him because [we] know his voice."[209] Listen to the voice of the Good Shepherd who has "the words of eternal life."[210]

When we follow Christ, we have eternal life. John 17:3 declares, "And this is the way to have eternal life—to know you, the only true God, and Jesus Christ, the one you sent."[211] If we desire to have eternal life, we need to stay with and know the Good Shepherd.

Elder John R. Lasater shared this story in general conference. While he was visiting Morocco, He was driving in a limousine with the King admiring the beautiful country. While they were driving, the limo driver accidentally struck and injured a sheep belonging to an old shepherd. The driver of the vehicle began to explain to Elder Lasater the law of the land. Because the King had injured a sheep, the shepherd was now entitled to one hundred times its value at maturity.

However, if the old shepherd accepted the compensation, under the same law, the injured sheep must be slain, and the meat divided among the people.

Elder Lasater was told that the old shepherd will not accept the money. They never do. Elder Laseter was startled and asked why. He was then told because of the love the shepherd has for the sheep, he will nurse it back to health rather than receive one-hundred times its value and have it killed.[212]

Like the Shepherds in Morocco, Jesus will never give us up no matter how injured we are. He will always take one broken sheep over one hundred new ones. He loves broken people. It brings Him joy to fix them.

As you think of our Good Shepherd, let us remember the wonderful words of the twenty-third Psalm, "The lord is my shepherd I shall not want. He maketh me to lie sown in green pastures: he leadeth me beside the still water. He restoreth my soul: he leadeth me in paths of righteousness for his name's sake. Yea, though I walk through the valley of the shadow of death, I will fear no evil for thou art with me; thy rod and staff they comfort me. Thou preparest a table before in the presence of my enemies: thou anointest my head with oil; my cup runneth over. Surely goodness and mercy will follow me the rest of my life: and I will dwell in the house of the lord for ever."

Jesus's name is Good Shepherd. Your new name is **found**. Jesus promises, "[You] will never be lost, and no one will tear [you] away from me."[213]

Governor

For out of thee shall come a Governor, that shall rule my people Israel.
Matthew 2:6, King James Version

A famous leader in the Old Testament is Joseph who was sold into Egypt by his brothers. After many hard years, Joseph became governor "over the land"[214] of Egypt and was able to save Egypt as well as his family from famine.

Joseph as the governor of Egypt is a type of Christ. If people didn't go to Joseph for food, they would perish. Likewise, if we don't go to our

Governor, Jesus Christ, we will perish. Jesus is the only person by whom we can obtain entrance into heaven.

In the U.S., we get to choose our leader by voting. Likewise, we can choose Jesus as our leader and let Him govern us. Jesus never forces people to join His team, but He accepts all who come unto Him.

As humans, we like to govern ourselves and try to do things on our own. However, we should choose Jesus and let Him govern us. Our role in bringing to pass good and achieving greatness is submitting to the will of God—to allow Him to utilize us as instruments in His hands.

Once we forget our will and desires and submit to the will and desire of the Lord, we will truly become great. C. S. Lewis taught, "Give up yourself, and you will find your real self. Lose your life and you will save it. Submit to death, death of your ambitions and favorite wishes every day and death of your whole body in the end: submit with every fiber of your being, and you will find eternal life. Keep back nothing. Nothing that you have not given away will ever be really yours. Nothing in you that has not died will ever be raised from the dead. Look for yourself, and you will find in the long run only hatred, loneliness, despair, rage, ruin, and decay. But look for Christ and you will find Him, and with Him everything else thrown in."[215]

You may now ask, if we all are doing the will of God are we not all exactly the same? No. Actually, coming to Jesus and turning our life over to him cultivates diversity. As we come to Christ, we find our true selves. We come to see how different we truly are.

Let's take power tools as an example. There are all kinds of power tools—drills, sanders, saws, etc. They are all tools, but each is very different. The difference between these tools is manifest when they are plugged into an outlet—the tools power source. When the tools are operating on electricity, they demonstrate how different they are. The sander smooths objects, the drill produces holes, and the saw cuts. Each is operating on the same power source, but each is very different.

Many seek an alternative power source. They try to operate according to their wills and desires. As we live on our own, the more dominated we become by our environment, upbringing, and natural desires. What we call "my desires" simply become the desires of the flesh—the desires of a natural man. As man submits to what he calls "his desires," he becomes much the same as the thousands of natural men who sought to fulfill their wills and desires.

"Sameness is to be found most among the most 'natural' men, not among those who surrender to Christ. How monotonously alike all the great tyrants and conquerors have been: how gloriously different are the saints . . . The more we get what we 'now call ourselves' out of the way and let Him take over, the more truly ourselves we become."[216]

We can have the most powerful and humble being as our leader—the Lord Jesus. He is a perfect Governor who wants us to have joy.[217]

Jesus's name is Governor. Your new name is **powerful**. As an instrument in the hands of Jesus, you have all power and "nothing will be impossible for you."[218]

Grace

For by grace are ye saved through faith; and that not of yourselves: it is the gift of God.
Ephesians 2:8, King James Version

I was blessed to grow up in a home where I was taught the good news that I am saved by my Savior's grace. I love teaching the good news of God's grace. However, when I teach that we are saved by grace, it is common for someone to chirp back, "Yeah, after all you can do."

It hurts my soul to see that some believe they are saved by works and thus don't fully receive Jesus's grace. When Jesus frees us from the pit of sin, this is called justification: declaring sinners perfect in Christ and holy even though there is still a gap between our performance and perfection. The gift of justification is instant when we put our faith and trust in Jesus. Once we have entered this saving relationship of being perfect in Christ, we then begin the process of sanctification, becoming perfect like Christ.

The scriptures make it clear, that salvation is a gift from Jesus, but some still don't understand the good news. Paul has clearly taught, "I have been crucified with Christ; yet I live; and yet no longer I, but Christ liveth in me: and that life which I now live in the flesh I live in faith, the faith which is in the Son of God, who loved me, and gave himself up for me . . . I do not frustrate the grace of God: for if righteousness is attainable by the law, then Christ hath died in vain."[219]

Jesus didn't come to suffer in the garden, hang on the cross, and rise again so we could work our way out of the pit of sin. That would ruin the whole point of Christ coming to redeem us. We don't do our share of the atonement or resurrection. Jesus did one hundred percent of it.

Jesus came because we couldn't do it on our own. He didn't come to give a boost or make up the difference. He came so He could carry us into the celestial kingdom. His love and grace are sufficient.[220]

While I was studying about this name, I had the impression to insert Jesus every time I saw the word 'grace'. As I did this, the Spirit was so strong. "For by [Jesus] are ye saved through faith."[221] "It is by [Jesus] that we are saved."[222]

When we declare that we are saved by grace, we are telling the whole world we are saved by Jesus. Grace isn't something that helps us. It is someone who is with us always. Grace isn't a thing that heals us. It's a person who binds our wounds. When we receive grace, we receive Jesus. Any help or assistance you feel, is from Jesus. "Jesus was the personification and the embodiment of grace . . . Jesus is the purpose and the point . . . No matter who you are or how badly you've messed up, grace and forgiveness are available in Jesus."[223]

Justification is an act of grace where Jesus declares the sinner holy, righteous, and not guilty instantly. The miracle of justification declares the imperfect as perfect *in* Christ and heirs of the celestial kingdom. You can learn more about grace in my book, *Perfect in Christ: The Good News of God's Grace,* and the book *Believing Christ* by Dr. Stephen E. Robinson.

Only through Jesus can we be healed. Only through Jesus can we be saved. Grace is our only option because Jesus is the only chance we have of gaining eternal life.

Jesus's name is Grace. Your new name is **justified**. You are perfect in Christ. You are holy, righteous, and not guilty. "All are justified freely by his grace through the redemption that came by Christ Jesus."[224] Jesus declares, "Your sins are forgiven you; you are clean before me; therefore, lift up your heads and rejoice."[225]

Mitchell C. Taylor

Great High Priest

Inasmuch . . . as we have in Jesus, the Son of God, a great High Priest who has passed into Heaven . . . let us hold firmly to our profession of faith.
Hebrews 4:14, Weymouth New Testament

During Old Testament times, people would make sacrifices in similitude of the great and last sacrifice of Jesus Christ. The people did these sacrifices to be pronounced clean in the sight of God. In addition to the individual sacrifices, a high priest would go into the Holy of Holies of the temple to offer a sacrifice for the sins of all people once a year.

No one was allowed to enter the Holy of Holies except the high priest. A veil covered the entrance to the temple's Holy of Holies. This veil represented our separation from God because of sin.

Only the high priest was permitted to enter the Holy of Holies. Absolutely no one else was allowed to pass through the veil into this part of the temple. Without the high priest offering a sacrifice on behalf of the people, they would be lost. The yearly sacrifice made by the high priest was symbolic of the great and last sacrifice to be completed by the Great High Priest—Jesus.

Amulek taught this doctrine, proclaiming, "Behold, I say unto you, that I do know that Christ shall come among the children of men, to take upon him the transgressions of his people, and that he shall atone for the sins of the world . . . For it is expedient that an atonement should be made . . . or else all mankind must unavoidably perish . . . For it is expedient that there should be a great and last sacrifice; yea, not a sacrifice . . . of beast . . . but it must be an infinite and eternal sacrifice . . . for the sins of the world . . . Then shall there be . . . a stop to the shedding of blood; then shall the law of Moses be fulfilled . . . And behold, this is the whole meaning of the law, every whit pointing to that great and last sacrifice; and that great and last sacrifice will be the Son of God, yea, infinite and eternal. And thus he shall bring salvation to all those who shall believe on his name."[226]

Jesus declares in Matthew 5:17, "Do not think that I have come to do away with the Law of Moses and the teachings of the prophets. I have not come to do away with them, but to make their teachings come true."[227] Jesus came to "fulfill all righteousness."[228]

Jesus suffered in the Garden of Gethsemane and died on the cross as the great and last sacrifice for our sins. Jesus satisfied justice once and for all. He is our Great High Priest.

When Jesus completed the sacrifice for sin, "the veil of the temple was torn in two from top to bottom."[229] Christ removed the veil so we no longer need a mortal high priest to enter the Holy of Holies, or God's presence, for us. Because of our Great High Priest, we can all enter the presence of God and "confidently approach the throne of grace to receive mercy and find grace whenever we need help."[230]

The apostle Paul wrote of Jesus's last and great sacrifice, "With his own blood—not the blood of goats and calves—he entered the Most Holy Place once for all time and secured our redemption forever."[231] Jesus was the only person who could enter the most holy place to make the sacrifice that saved us all.

Jesus's name is Great High Priest. Your new name is **worthy**. Jesus has wrapped you in His "robe of righteousness."[232] He has "accounted [you] worthy"[233] to "enter into the joy of your lord."[234] "Be of good cheer, for . . . the kingdom is yours and the blessings thereof are yours, and the riches of eternity are yours."[235]

Greater

Greater is He who is in you than he who is in the world.
1 John 4:4, Berean Study Bible

One of my favorite parables taught by Jesus is that of the Pharisee and the publican. The story goes as follows: "Two men went to the Temple to pray. One was a proud, self-righteous Pharisee, and the other a cheating tax collector. The proud Pharisee 'prayed' this prayer: 'Thank God, I am not a sinner like everyone else, especially like that tax collector over there! For I never cheat, I don't commit adultery, I go without food twice a week, and I give to God a tenth of everything I earn.' But the corrupt tax collector stood at a distance and dared not even lift his eyes to heaven as he prayed, but beat upon his chest in sorrow, exclaiming, 'God, be merciful to me, a sinner.' I tell you, this sinner, not the Pharisee, returned home forgiven! For the proud shall be humbled, but the humble shall be honored."[236]

In order to gain a better understanding of this story, we need to remember who Jesus was teaching. The Bible tells us Jesus was teaching those who were "complacently pleased with themselves over their moral performance and looked down their noses at the common people."[237]

Some will view themselves greater than others because of their commandment keeping or their obedience to the law. But in reality, we are nothing. Only one person can claim to be greater, and that person is Jesus.

To be in a proper relationship with Jesus, we must recognize our carnal and fallen state, which is less than the dust of the earth. We should cry aloud, "O have mercy, and apply the atoning blood of Christ that we may receive forgiveness of our sins, and our hearts may be purified; for we believe in Jesus Christ, the Son of God, who created heaven and earth, and all things."[238]

Every one of us is no greater than the dust of the earth, yet we still place ourselves in categories of righteousness based on our works and merits. We aren't the ones to judge who is higher quality dirt. We should acknowledge our unworthiness before God at all times.[239]

God sent Jesus, who is greater than the world, to overcome sin and death. Without Jesus, we are nothing but dirt. With Jesus, we are greater than all things. Without Jesus, "[we] can do nothing."[240] With Jesus, we can do the impossible.

We don't become great by our works and merits. We become great by coming to the One who is Great and Mighty. Only through the merits, mercy, and grace of Jesus do we become great.

We all are able to overcome the world because of the One who is Greater—Jesus. The apostle John teaches, "Who is it that overcomes the world? Only the one who believes that Jesus is the Son of God."[241]

Jesus's name is Greater. Your new name is **overcomer**. "For everyone born of God is victorious and overcomes the world."[242] "It is finished; it is finished! The Lamb of God hath overcome and trodden the wine-press alone, even the wine-press of the fierceness of the wrath of Almighty God."[243] Jesus declares, "I have told you these things, so that in Me you may have [perfect] peace. In the world you have tribulation and distress and suffering, but be courageous [be confident, be undaunted, be filled with joy]; I have overcome the world."[244] "God is greater."[245]

Holy, Holy, Holy

Holy, holy, holy is the LORD Almighty; the whole earth is full of his glory.
Isaiah 6:3, New International Version

The word 'holy' is used over six hundred times in the scriptures. The use of the word 'holy' is a very meaningful and powerful concept. 'Holy' is used to describe someone who is pure, set apart, and sanctified. In Hebrew, when something is said three times in a row, it means it is extremely important. Jesus repeats the words, "Verily, verily,"[246] to get our attention. The repetition of words is used to add emphasis, meaning, and power.

The repetition of words 'holy, holy' in reference to the Holiness of God shows that His Holiness is above and beyond any earthly concept of holiness. Jesus is holier than holy.

The repeating of the word 'holy' three times is an act of total praise and worship. It is a powerful declaration of God's holiness and perfection and our total dependence on Him. It is a recognition that there is only one who is "Holy, Holy, Holy."[247]

1 Peter 1:16 teaches, "You must be holy because I am holy."[248] Jesus is the standard we want to meet, but we constantly sin and fall short of the glory of God.[249] Jesus can't "look upon sin with the least degree of allowance"[250] so to enter the kingdom of God, we must be holy like Him.

How do we obtain this holiness? It is impossible to become holy by the law. If we try to become holy by perfectly keeping **all** the laws, we will fail miserably. It is important to keep the law, but the only way to become holy is through Jesus, the Holy One. Only He can declare us holy like Him. We are made holy by the Holy, Holy, Holy One.

Jesus's name is Holy, Holy, Holy. Your new name is **blameless**. When you are in a relationship with Jesus, He declares you "blameless and holy in the presence of . . . God."[251]

Mitchell C. Taylor

Hope

Our Savior, and Lord Jesus Christ, who is our hope.
1 Timothy 1:1, Webster's Bible Translation

In *Star Wars: A New Hope*, Princess Leia sends a distress message to Obi-Wan saying, "Help me, Obi-Wan Kenobi. You are my only hope."

We all desperately need hope. Pastor Rick Warren taught, "You can survive forty days without food, three days without water, and eight minutes without air. But you can't last a single second without hope. It's an essential part of life. When hope is gone, life is over." Without hope, the waves of life "toss . . . [us] back and forth,"[252] and we want to abandon ship. When hope is lost, we want to curl up in a ball, cry, and give up.

Where can we find lasting hope? There is always hope in the Lord Jesus Christ. Jesus is our Hope. When we put our faith and trust in Jesus, we can have a "perfect brightness of hope"[253] and know that we are saved. Hope comes from the Holy One of Hope—Jesus. Any other source "is a false hope for salvation."[254] Jesus is our only chance. Trust in the Hope of the world and be saved.

Without the great and atoning sacrifice of Jesus, all hope would be lost. We would have no chance of returning to live with God. Jesus died to give us a "lively hope."[255] Because Jesus laid down His life, there is hope for sinners like you and me. Jesus gives us a perfect "hope of eternal life."[256]

Jesus wants you to know that you are saved through His redeeming blood. When you accept Jesus as your hope for salvation, "you will overflow with hope"[257] and know you are saved!

Look steadfastly to Jesus, your only source of hope, and plead as did Princess Leia, "Help me, Jesus. You are my only hope."

Jesus's name is Hope. Your new name is **hopeful**. All who take "upon them . . . the name of Christ . . . are saved by hope."[258] You can say with confidence, "I know I am saved, because 'I know in whom I have trusted.'"[259]

Whom Say Ye that I Am?

I AM

I Am who I Am.
Exodus 3:14, Christian Standard Bible

After Moses fled Egypt, he stayed in hiding for many years. When the time was right, the Lord appeared to Moses in a burning bush. He commanded Moses saying, "Therefore, go! I am sending you to Pharaoh to bring My people the Israelites out of Egypt."[260]

Moses asked the Lord, "If I come to the people of Israel and say to them, 'The God of your fathers has sent me to you,' and they ask me, 'What is his name?' what shall I say to them?"[261] Then "God replies to Moses, 'I Am who I Am. This is what you are to say to the Israelites: I Am has sent me to you.'"[262]

The name the Lord gave to Moses in Hebrew is '*ehyeh*. The word '*ehyeh* is the first-person form of *hayah*, "to be," and means "I am."[263]

When Jesus speaks, He talks in the present tense. All things are present before the Lord. He is the God who was, who is, and ever shall be. He is the great I Am.

Jesus declares, "All things are present before mine eyes."[264] We are eternal beings with no beginning and no end. There is no past. There is no future. All things are present. Life is to be enjoyed in each moment of now. The idea of a past and a future is a temporary illusion of mortality. Living in the present is key to joyful living.

One of my favorite scriptures is, "Men [and women] are, that they might have joy."[265] The words "are" and "have" are present tense. We are to have joy now. Joy is not a future state to achieve. Joy is not a reward to receive after years of work or a gift reserved for the next life. We are to experience the glad tidings of great joy *now*. To enjoy the present, you must let go of the pains and guilt of the past and eliminate the worries of the future.

The Lord teaches in the Sermon on the Mount, "Take therefore no thought for the morrow: for the morrow shall take thought for the things of itself."[266] This scripture is confusing to some, but it's easy to understand when you know how to live in the present. Another translation of this verse reads, "So don't be anxious about tomorrow. God will take care of your tomorrow too. Live one day at a time."[267]

God is directing us to live in the present. He created you to have joy now. When you live with joy, you fulfill the measure of your creation.

Throughout Jesus's mortal ministry, He used the phrase "I Am" to express His relationship with us. He states:

"I am the bread of life (John 6:35)."

"I am the light of the world (John 8:12)."

"I am the door of the sheep (John 10:7)."

"I am the good shepherd (John 10:11)."

"I am the resurrection and the life (John 11:25)."

"I am the way, the truth, and the life (John 14:6)."

"I am the true vine (John 15:1)."

When we hear these names, we are reminded that Jesus is our salvation. He is our light to guide us. He is our food and water. He is the shepherd who protects us, and we look to Him for truth.

Because Jesus is the great I Am, we can declare in the present tense:

I am nourished.

I am directed.

I am protected.

Jesus performed countless miracles as a part of His mortal ministry. John 21:25 declares, "Jesus also did many other things. If every one of them were written down, I suppose the world wouldn't have enough room for the books that would be written."[268]

Jesus healed the sick, gave sight to the blind, and raised the dead, but His greatest miracle is forgiving sins. As soon as "you openly declare that Jesus is Lord and believe in your heart that God raised him from the dead,"[269] Jesus says, "Friend, your sins are forgiven."[270]

Jesus never says, "Your sins can be," or "Your sins will be forgiven." He declares in the present tense, "Your sins *are* forgiven."[271] You are saved and forgiven now! Not tomorrow, not ten years from now, not when you are good enough. "Everyone who calls on the name of the Lord will be saved."[272] Jesus has paid the price for your forgiveness; you just need to accept His gift and follow Him. You are saved and forgiven *now*!

Because Jesus is the great I Am, you can declare in the present tense:

I am saved.

I am forgiven.

Whom Say Ye that I Am?

Jesus's name is I Am. Your new name is **forgiven**. Jesus suffered in Gethsemane, hung on the cross, and was resurrected so He could call you by name and say, "Your sins are forgiven."[273]

Immanuel

*Behold, a virgin shall conceive, and bear a son,
and shall call his name Immanuel.*
Isaiah 7:14, King James Version

My freshman year of high school, I made the school basketball team, but my teammates treated me like an outsider. They ignored and made fun of me because I was homeschooled. I had been homeschooled since the third grade and have loved every minute of it. I was hoping my teammates would be my friends, but instead, they totally disregarded me.

Many feel like I did my freshman year—alone, mistreated, and forgotten. They go through life believing they are nothing and everyone is against them. They feel lost and surrounded by immense darkness. No matter how unloved you feel or how "lost and homeless"[274] you are, Jesus is *always* by your side.

'Immanuel' means God with us or God is with us. This name is a reminder that Jesus is always with you. When we sing *O Come, O Come, Emmanuel*, we are beckoning Jesus into our lives. Jesus is crazy about you and wants to be with you. You just open the door and let Him in.

Jesus decided to be born in the lowliest of circumstances. He could have been born in a castle, have high status, and lived as a king, but He chose to be born in a manager, in a cave, to a peasant. Instead of living like royalty, He chose to be with us, a bunch of sinners. He was willing to give up His high status to be with you and me. He chose to come as Immanuel.

No matter who you are, no matter what you've done, Jesus wants to be with you. He loves you so much that He has "engraved you on the palms of [His] hands."[275] He is your best friend. "He will be with you; he will not leave you or forsake you."[276] He promises, "I am with you always."[277]

No matter what you are going through, no matter your circumstances, Jesus is with you. He will deliver you.

Even though we live in a world of pain, despair, loss, doubt, fear, and chaos, Immanuel is always by our side comforting and strengthening us. You don't need to be afraid because Jesus is with you. He is your friend and is by your side the whole time. "He is a God with you."[278]

Jesus's name is Immanuel. Your new name is **precious**. Jesus is with you always. Jesus's words to you are these, "You are precious to me . . . I love you."[279]

Jesus

And, behold, thou shalt conceive in thy womb, and bring forth a son, and shalt call his name Jesus.
Luke 1:31, King James Version

When we are born, our parents give us a name. Sometimes we are named after a family member or a good friend. I'm named after my dad's business partner and friend, Mitch Huhem. My name is derived from the name Michael, which means "who is like God." Names have special meaning, and the reason Jesus was called Jesus is absolutely amazing.

The name 'Jesus' in the Bible is usually translated from the word *Yeshuah*, which is the Hebrew word for salvation. Jesus is salvation. There is only one place to find salvation and it's Jesus. Acts 4:12 declares, "There is salvation in no one else! God has given no other name under heaven by which we must be saved."[280] There is only one source for our salvation, and it's in our best friend, Jesus.

In Greek, the name 'Jesus' is *Joshua* or *Jeshua*, which means God is help or God is salvation. This meaning is in the present tense on purpose. Jesus's name isn't "God will help you" or "God might save you." God is your salvation. He is your help. Jesus promises in Isaiah 41:10, "Don't be afraid, because I'm with you; don't be anxious, because I am your God. I keep on strengthening you; I'm truly helping you. I'm surely upholding you with my victorious right hand."[281] Jesus is your help. He is always by your side. He loves you.

The Hebrew word *Yeshuah* can also mean "to rescue." In Hebrew culture, "a name was a representation of whom the individual was based on

His character and function."[282] Jesus came to rescue the lost.[283] He came to rescue us from sin and death. His mission was to rescue us! What better name to give the Son of God than rescuer!

Our Lord's name is Jesus. Your new name is **rescued**. Jesus conquered sin and death. He has promised, "I will save you from the hands of the wicked . . . I will rescue you."[284]

Jesus of Nazareth, Nazarene

Whom seek ye? And they said, Jesus of Nazareth.
John 18:7, King James Version

During New Testament time, people were referred to by the city they grew up in or by their father's name. It was prophesied that Jesus would be called a Nazarene.[285] Despite not having been born there, He was identified as one from Nazareth, one of the lowliest places on earth. A common saying during Jesus's life was, "Nothing good can come from Nazareth."[286] Our Savior, the Supreme Being of the universe, would be called Jesus of Nazareth. He went from the highest to the lowest.

One of my favorite stories is found in John 18:4-6. Jesus is about to be arrested by the Sanhedrin and tried for blasphemy for claiming to be God. Jesus had suffered in Gethsemane for the sins of the world and a mob came to sentence Him to death.

When the mob approached, Jesus asked, "Whom seek ye?"[287] The mob replies, "Jesus of Nazareth."[288] Jesus answers, "I am he."[289] As soon as Jesus spoke these three words, "they went backward, and fell to the ground."[290]

His name had so much power that the mob was thrown to the ground. Jesus also healed Malchus's ear after Peter cut it off with a sword.[291] However, the mob was unchanged by these miracles. When Jesus was taken to Pilate, they demanded their Savior be killed, yelling, "Crucify Him! Crucify Him!"[292]

The mob calling for Christ's crucifixion only saw a man from Nazareth who challenged their culture and told them to repent of their wrongdoings. They were blinded by ego and killed their Redeemer.

Do you see Jesus as a Nazarene or as the promised Messiah who was foretold to redeem Israel? The Pharisees couldn't see Him for who He is, but you can. Jesus is the Savior of the world. He died so you can be forgiven. He came to save you. He is the Messiah.

You might feel hopeless and believe there is no chance for you. You might think nothing good can come of your life. But I have good news for you! Jesus of Nazareth can turn every situation one hundred eighty degrees. He makes beauty from ashes.[293] Nothing is impossible for Jesus of Nazareth.

With three words, Jesus of Nazareth threw the mob to the ground. At His word, Jesus of Nazareth can drive away your fear, anxiety, stress, and doubt. No matter how big the worry, no matter how big the pain, it must all submit to Jesus.

Jesus's name is Nazarene. Your new name is **assured**. You can have "great assurance in [your] faith in Christ Jesus"[294] because He "never fails."[295] Nothing can stop an unstoppable God.

Judge

For he cometh to judge the earth: he shall judge the world with righteousness, and the people with his truth.
Psalm 96:13, King James Version

When someone is charged with committing a crime, they go before a judge to determine their guilt or innocence. When we die, we will appear before the judgment bar. Do you want to be judged fairly? If you answered yes, congratulations, you are going to hell. We all are sinners who are "consigned to a state of endless wo."[296] If we are judged fairly, the gavel will slam with a guilty verdict.

Only those who are perfect can be saved, which is none of us, for "there is no one who is righteous."[297] To go to the celestial kingdom, we need a judge who can satisfy the law and also give us a not-guilty verdict. Luckily, we have Jesus, the perfect Judge on our side.

Whom Say Ye that I Am?

The word 'judge' comes from the Hebrew word *dyin,* which means to bring life to another. In Hebrew, judge "is used as a legal term but not in the modern Western sense of seeking guilt or condemnation. Rather it is seeking innocence or life."[298]

Jesus has no desire to condemn us. He is our friend. He is by our side fighting for our innocence. Jesus "is not a heartless referee looking for any excuse to"[299] give us a guilty verdict. "He . . . yearns more than anything else to have [us] come back home and live with Him."[300] He is a merciful judge who is going to do whatever it takes to declare us not guilty.

However, Jesus must uphold the law. The Book of Mormon declares, "Now the work of justice could not be destroyed; if so, God would cease to be God."[301] To satisfy the demands of justice, Jesus took the condemnation upon Himself so we wouldn't have too.[302]

Jesus paid the price, satisfied the law, and declared us free—not because we deserved it, but because He "loved us."[303] When we are with Christ, the law is upheld, and we are saved.

Jesus and Heavenly Father knew that "all have sinned and fall short of the glory of God,"[304] but Heavenly Father had a plan. His plan is beautifully laid out in John 3:16–17. "For God so loved the world that he gave his only begotten son, that whosoever believeth in him should not perish, but have everlasting life. For God sent not his Son into the world to condemn the world; but that the world through him might be saved." Heavenly Father gave us His Son, Jesus Christ, so we could be perfect in Christ and declared "not guilty."

Jesus's love and grace covers all the mistakes we have ever made. We sin. We deny Him. We forget Him. We underestimate Him. The list goes on, but "where sin was powerful, God's gift of undeserved grace was even more powerful."[305]

Jesus loves you so much that He was willing to give His life for you. The power is in His hands to determine where you will go. If you believe in Him, He will declare you not guilty and give you the gift of eternal life.

Jesus's name is Judge. Your new name is **not guilty**. Jesus "was wounded and bruised for *our* sins. He was beaten that we might have peace; he was lashed—and we were healed . . . No condemnation . . . exists for those in Christ Jesus."[306]

Mitchell C. Taylor

Keeper of the Gate

. . . the keeper of the gate is the Holy One of Israel; and he employeth no servant there; and there is none other way save it be by the gate.
2 Nephi 9:41

When you go to an elegant party or dinner, you have to be on the guest list to go in. You can try as hard as you want to get in—sneak, dig, climb, maybe even bribe—but if you aren't on the list, you don't get in. Many who want to go to the party or dinner are excluded with no way to enter. Only a special few are invited.

Sometimes I feel we put this same parameter on our access to heaven. That only a special few will be able to enter and enjoy the party of heaven. However, the Guard in front of heaven wants everyone to come in. 2 Nephi 26:33 states, that Jesus ". . . inviteth them all to come unto him and partake of his goodness." Jesus invites everyone to His heavenly party.

There is only one way into heaven and it's through the gate. You can't climb, dig, sneak, or bribe your way in. But how do we get through the gate? We have to be in a relationship with the Gatekeeper. He determines who goes in.

Baptism is referred to as the gate to the covenant path. It is the ordinance that declares us perfect in Christ and we enter a relationship with Jesus. If we want to return to God, we must have a relationship with the Gatekeeper.

Jesus wants all of us to come home and be with Him. Jesus gave His life for you. If you are in a relationship with Jesus, you are on the list and you are admitted to the celestial kingdom. "He denieth none that come unto him."[307]

If we keep the commandments, serve others, perform miracles in His name, but don't know Jesus, He will declare, "Ye never knew me: depart from me, ye that work iniquity."[308] Having a relationship with Jesus is the only way to pass through the gate into the celestial kingdom.

Jesus's name is Keeper of the Gate. Your new name is **admitted**. Jesus urges all to "Come to [Him],"[309] and He denies none.[310]

Whom Say Ye that I Am?

King

And he hath on his vesture and on his thigh a name written, KING OF KINGS.
Revelation 19:16, King James Version

When we hear the word 'king', our minds think of someone high in power and ruling over a people. Having a king can be good, but it can also be bad. Some kings put burdensome taxes upon the people so they can live a life of luxury and ease.

We don't want a king like King Noah, who focuses on himself. We want a king like King Benjamin and King Mosiah, who work alongside the people. In Hebrew the word king comes from the word *melek*, which means a mighty one walks.

A king isn't supposed to sit on a throne, secluded from his people. He is to walk with his people and be one of them. Jesus isn't a king who sits on His throne and leaches off his people. He is one who walks alongside us.

King Mosiah taught His people to enter "into a covenant with God"[311] and to "put [their] trust in the Lord."[312] Our King, Jesus Christ, makes covenants with us, His people. When we make a covenant with Christ to follow Him, He promises to take care of us.

Being in a covenant relationship with King Jesus is the greatest thing ever, but some misunderstand the criteria to be in a covenant relationship with Christ. Often when we see the words "keep and break," we assume "obedience=keep" and "disobedience=break." We are all sinners and disobedient to commandments every day, so if disobedience caused us to break our covenant with Christ, nobody would ever be in a covenant relationship with Jesus.

In Hebrew the word for keep is *shamar*, which means to guard.
> The original use of this word is a corral constructed out of thorn bushes by the shepherd to protect his flock from predators during the night. The shamar was built to "guard" the flock . . . We now see that "keeping the covenant" is not strictly about obedience, but "guarding the covenant." The individual's attitude toward the covenant is the issue, does he guard it as a shepherd does his flock, or does he "break" the covenant.[313]

The word 'break' in Hebrew is *parar*, which means trample. We don't break our covenant with God when we are disobedient. It is all about our attitude toward our relationship with Jesus. So "the keeping and breaking of a covenant is the respect, or lack of, that one has for the covenant."[314] Jesus has told us that the requirement to be in a covenant relationship with Him is "a broken heart and a contrite spirit."[315]

Jesus teaches this repeatedly in the scriptures. In the Old Testament, it reads, "The Lord is nigh unto them that are of a broken heart; and saveth such as be of a contrite spirit."[316]

The Book of Mormon teaches, "Redemption cometh in and through the Holy Messiah; for he is full of grace and truth. Behold, he offereth himself a sacrifice for sin, to answer the ends of the law, unto all those who have a broken heart and a contrite spirit; and unto none else can the ends of the law be answered."[317]

The Doctrine and Covenants declares, "Jesus was crucified . . . for the sins of the world, yea, for the remission of sins unto the contrite heart."[318]

Jesus wants to be in a covenant relationship with you. He wants your heart. He desires to stay with you. The only way to leave the covenant with Jesus is to no longer want to be with Jesus. King Jesus will never kick you out. You have to choose to leave.

Jesus is a supreme being of the universe. He is royalty and king over all, yet He descended below everything. He became a peasant. He had the power to save all mankind but never acted greater than the lowest publican. He never boasted Himself above another. He only cared for the welfare of His friends.

Jesus is the greatest, most powerful person to ever walk the earth, but He used that power to save us from sin. Jesus taught, "Whoever is the greatest should be the servant of the others."[319] Most kings abuse their power to gain status, riches, and wealth, but "He gave his life to free us from every kind of sin, to cleanse us, and to make us his very own people."[320]

Jesus is a king of uncountable worlds.[321] He is the King of Kings. We are His children and heirs to all that He has.[322] We are princes and princesses to inherit all things. Jesus doesn't just want you to be a subject in His kingdom. He wants you to be a king or queen with Him in the celestial kingdom. "The children of Christ [are] heirs to the kingdom of God."[323]

Whom Say Ye that I Am?

Jesus's name is King. Your new name is **heir**. Jesus has chosen us "to be rich in faith and heirs of the kingdom."[324] "We . . . become heirs *of all things* . . . because of an overflowing hope of eternal life."[325]

Lamb of God

Behold the Lamb of God.[326]
—John the Baptist (John 1:29 King James Version)

In the Bible, Abraham wanted to be a father so badly. He cried to the Lord saying, "LORD All-Powerful, you have given me everything I could ask for, except children."[327] The Lord blessed Abraham with a son named Isaac.[328] Abraham loved his son, but the Lord commanded Abraham to perform an unbearable task. God said to Abraham, "Go get Isaac, your only son, the one you dearly love! Take him to the land of Moriah, and I will show you a mountain where you must sacrifice him to me on the fires of an altar."[329]

Abraham didn't want to sacrifice his only son, but he obeyed the command of the Lord. "Abraham rose up early in the morning, and saddled his ass, and took two of his young men with him, and Isaac his son, and clave the wood for the burnt offering, and rose up, and went unto the place of which God had told him."[330]

After a long journey, they reached the top of the mountain. Isaac asked, "Behold the fire and the wood: but where is the lamb for a burnt offering?"[331] Abraham answered, "God will provide himself a lamb for a burnt offering."[332]

Abraham laid Isaac across the altar to slay him and Isaac didn't resist. He laid still understanding what must be done, but before Abraham killed his son, an angel appeared and commanded, "Don't lay a hand on the boy! . . . Do not hurt him in any way, for now I know that you truly fear God. You have not withheld from me even your son, your only son."[333]

After the angel left, "Abraham looked up and saw a ram caught in the thicket by its horns. So Abraham went and took the ram and offered as a burnt offering in place of his son."[334]

Before the atonement of our Lord, people offered sacrifices to make themselves right and clean in the eyes of God. They offered their best and unblemished lamb to represent the atoning sacrifice of Jesus Christ. Luckily, this isn't the case anymore. Jesus has taken our place on the altar. He is our ram in the thicket. He atoned so we "might not suffer . . . even as [He did]."[335]

Jesus made the once and for all sacrifice for every one of us. We no longer have to sacrifice a lamb because the Lamb of God has fulfilled all righteousness. We don't have to make an atonement ourselves because "if our sins have been forgiven and forgotten . . . there is no need to offer any more sacrifices."[336]

Christ has offered His "life to rescue many people."[337] "The Lamb of God hath overcome and trodden the wine-press alone . . . It is finished. It is finished!"[338]

While Adam and Eve were in the garden, they were "in a state of innocence . . . doing no good, for they knew no sin."[339] Once they partook of the forbidden fruit, they had to leave the presence of God, but before they were evicted from the presence of God, the Lord clothed them in "coats of skins."[340]

Likewise, we are sinners and unable to be in the presence of God, but Jesus wraps us in His, "robe of righteousness."[341] Jesus justifies us, making us righteous and holy in the sight of God.

Jesus wants you to return to His presence. He was willing to be your ram in the thicket. He is your friend who atoned in Gethsemane. He is your Redeemer who hung on the cross for you! Look to the Lamb of God, put on His "robe of righteousness,"[342] and be saved.

Jesus's name is Lamb of God. Your new name is **clean**. You are "righteous forever . . . because of [your] faith in the Lamb of God [and your] garments are made white in his blood."[343]

Lawgiver

The LORD is our lawgiver . . . He will save us.
Isaiah 33:22, King James Version

We are very familiar with laws and commandments that we follow every day of our lives—driving the speed limit, not killing people, not shoplifting, etc. These laws are in place to protect our God-given rights "of life, liberty, and the pursuit of happiness."[344] Without the law, there is no freedom. The Lord declares in the Doctrine and Covenants, "Hear my voice and follow me, and you shall be a free people . . . I am your lawgiver."[345]

Whenever the Lord commands us to do something, we can know that it "shall give thee experience and shall be for thy good"[346] because "all things have been done in the wisdom of Him who knoweth all things."[347] When a law is infringed, there are negative consequences. God has laws in place to guide and protect us.

Jesus invites us saying, "Come follow me." When we choose to follow Jesus, we become his disciples. A disciple is a student or follower of a leader or teacher. As a disciple of Jesus, we strive to do what he asks and seek to become like Him.

Jesus commands, "If you love me, you will obey my commandments."[348] We show our love to God and our desire to follow Him by obeying Him, but we need to keep obeying the law in its proper place.

We cannot put the law above our lawgiver—Jesus. The law was given to help us come closer to Jesus and recognize our nothingness before Him. Mosiah 13:29–30 states, "And now I say unto you that it was expedient that there should be a law given . . . yea, even a very strict law; for they were a stiffnecked people, quick to do iniquity, and slow to remember the Lord their God; Therefore there was a law given them, yea, a law of performances and of ordinances, a law which they were to observe strictly from day to day, to keep them in remembrance of God and their duty towards him."

The law is given to help us remember Jesus and His central role in our lives. We can follow the law but miss the whole point of the law, which is to bring us closer to Jesus.

The Pharisees were incredible at keeping the law. They fasted twice a week, paid their tithes, and served, but they weren't born again. Their hearts didn't change. They emphasized the law so profusely that it became their savior. They wanted to be saved by the law. They rejected the Lawgiver and His gift of salvation. The law isn't a list of dos and don'ts in order to get into heaven and be found worthy; rather, it is a guide to help us become like Jesus. The law is supposed to help us come unto Christ and gain His characteristics.

During His ministry to the Nephites, Jesus told them, "I am the law."[349] Everything in the law emulates a part of His perfectness. While Jesus is the lawgiver, He is also the law keeper. He won't tell us to do something He isn't already doing. He keeps all the laws perfectly and never waivers. As we keep the law, we will become more like Jesus, the perfect law keeper. We grow "brighter and brighter until the perfect day."[350] "As the Spirit of the Lord works within [you, you] become more and more like him."[351]

Jesus's name is Lawgiver. Your new name is **disciple**. Jesus says to those who believe, "If you . . . follow my teaching, you are . . . my disciples and you will know the truth, and the truth will set you free."[352]

Light of the World

I am the light of the world: he that followeth me shall not walk in darkness, but shall have the light of life.[353]
—Jesus (John 8:12, King James Version)

When I was a kid, I was very afraid of the dark. I was scared of the boogie man, monsters in my closet, and creatures under my bed. I worried a creature was going to snatch me from my bed. I remember on one occasion waking up in the middle of the night when it was super dark. I contemplated whether to make a bolt for the door to go to my parents' room for refuge.

I eventually built up the courage to rush to the door, but I tripped over some toys on the ground and became lost. I couldn't find the light switch or the door so I went to a light I could find—a small light coming from the on button of the desktop computer tower. I curled up into a ball next to the small light underneath the desk.

As I cried, a miracle occurred. My mom came into the room and turned on the light. I was saved! I rushed to my mom and gave her the biggest hug ever. My mom and the light saved me from the darkness.

Jesus is the Light that saves us from darkness. Jesus is the Light of the World. When light enters, darkness vanishes. "Whoever follows [Jesus] will have the light of life and will never walk in darkness."[354]

When we are lost, afraid, or in darkness, we can turn to Jesus as our beacon of light, hope, and safety. Jesus "is a lamp for [our] feet, a light on [our] path."[355]

Light also reveals things that are hidden. Light is an agent that stimulates sight and makes things visible. Light allows us to see what is hidden in darkness. Jesus "knows all hidden things, for he is light, and darkness is no obstacle to him."[356]

Light also promotes growth and life. Plants, trees, and humans get vitamins from the sun. Without the sun, life shrivels up and dies. Likewise, without the light of Jesus, life shrivels up and dies. Jesus is our exclusive source of light and life.

Jesus's name is Light of the World. Your new name is **conqueror**. Light conquerors darkness. All who have "faith in the name of Jesus . . . come off conqueror . . . and . . . escape the hands of . . . Satan."[357] Jesus conquers Satan. The Light of the World wins! In the battle between Jesus and Satan, good and evil, light and darkness, the question is not who will win but whose side you are on.

Lion of the Tribe of Judah

Stop weeping! Look, the Lion of the tribe of Judah . . . has won the victory.
Revelations 5:5, New Living Translation

The name 'Lion of the Tribe of Judah' was given to John the Revelator in a vision while he was in prison on the island of Patmos. John recorded this vision in the book of Revelation. The vision starts with an angel proclaiming, "Who is worthy to break the seals and open the scroll?"[358] "But no one in heaven or on earth or under the earth was able to open the scroll and read it."[359]

Absolutely nobody is found worthy to open the scrolls and "[John] began to weep loudly."[360] As John was crying, an elder came to his side and proclaims, "Stop weeping! Look, the Lion of the tribe of Judah, the heir to David's throne, has won the victory. He is worthy to open the scroll and its seven seals."[361]

When John heard this, I can see him saying, "Hallelujah, The Lion has saved us!" When John looked to see the lion, he "saw a Lamb standing, as though it had been slain."[362] This imagery may be a bit confusing. "Where is the strong lion? How in the world can a weak little lamb save us?"

Jesus is the Lion who came in the form of a lamb to save us from sin. A lion is symbolic of royalty, majesty, strength, and courage. Jesus is this lion, but He is also the lamb.

Because Jesus was willing to "descended below…all [things]"[363] and become a sacrificial lamb, He can lift us to unimaginable heights. "Worthy is the lamb who was killed to receive power and wealth and wisdom and might and honor and glory and praise!"[364] His worthiness saves us. His perfection cleanses us. "The Lion . . . has won the victory. He is worthy."[365] Jesus is the Lion and the Lamb who understands you perfectly.

Jesus's name is Lion of the Tribe of Judah. Your new name is **understood**. Jesus has "drunk out of . . . the bitter cup . . . that his bowels may be filled with mercy, according to the flesh, that he may know according to the flesh how to succor his people."[366]

LORD

Believe in the Lord Jesus and you will be saved.
Acts 16:31, New Living Translation

Jesus declares in the book of Isaiah, "I am the Lord: that is my name."[367] We are familiar with Jesus's name 'Lord', but we may not fully understand why He is called Lord. In Hebrew, the word for Lord is *adon*, which means one who brings life, the deliverer. In Hebrew culture, the head of the house was the *adon*. All power was in their hands, and they did what they thought was best for their family.

Jesus is the *adon* of all creation.[368] Under the direction of God the Father, He is over all. He is over you, and He is over me. Nothing is outside His power and control. Even though Jesus has all power and authority, we still try to do things by ourselves and trust in our own efforts. Jesus "has been placed above all rule and authority and—by virtue of who He is—demands first place."[369] What He says goes, and what He commands is done.

Whom Say Ye that I Am?

Jesus should be at the helm of your life, leading and guiding you. Jesus should be the Lord of your life.

In Hebrew culture, it was customary for the lord—*adon*—to give new names to the people he was over. When Daniel and His friends were taken captive by the Babylonians, King Nebuchadnezzar gave them each a new name.[370] God changed Abram's name to Abraham.[371] He changed Jacob's name to Israel,[372] and Saul's name was changed to Paul.[373]

When we enter a covenant relationship with the Lord, He gives us a new name to show that we are no longer under the world but under Him. We have a new Lord and Master. Jesus changes our names to show a change in lordship.

When you accept Jesus as the Lord, *adon*, of your life, He gives you a new name and waits to take you to eternal life.

Jesus's name is Lord. Your new name is **secure**. With Jesus as the Lord of your life, you can declare with confidence, "I am saved."[374] "Everyone who calls on the name of the Lord will be saved."[375]

Lord of Hosts

Holy, holy, holy, is the Lord of hosts: the whole earth is full of his glory.
Isaiah 6:3, King James Version

In the Bible, the Syrians feared Elisha because of the power he possessed from God. They wanted to destroy him. One day the servant of Elisha woke up and saw the Syrian's gigantic army approaching and ran to Elisha saying, "Alas, my master! What shall we do?"[376] Elisha calmly answered, "Don't be afraid . . . For our army is bigger than theirs!"[377]

The young servant was confused. He didn't see any army to deliver them. They were going to die. "Elisha prayed, 'O Lord, open his eyes and let him see!' The Lord opened the young man's eyes, and when he looked up, he saw that the hillside around Elisha was filled with horses and chariots of fire."[378]

The name, Lord of Hosts, is translated from the Hebrew words *adoni tzva'ot*, which mean "Lord of armies." When you are on Jesus's team, you will never be outnumbered "because greater is He who is in you than he who is in the world."[379] When you are with Jesus, you will always be greater than your enemy. "The army that fights for us is larger than the one against us."[380]

When Hannah was unable to have children, she knew that the God of heavenly armies and the commander of all things could heal her. She prayed, "Lord of Hosts . . . give Your servant a son."[381] The Lord of Hosts answered her prayer, and she became the mother of the prophet Samuel. Every atom, molecule, and angel moved in accordance with God's purposes.

Jesus's name is Lord of Hosts. Your new name is **protected**. Jesus has an army surrounding you on all sides. He promises, "I will go before your face. I will be on your right and on your left, and my spirit shall be in your hearts, and my angels round about you, to bear you up."[382] "Lord, those who know your name come to you for protection."[383]

Lord of the Sabbath

For the Son of Man is Lord of the Sabbath.
Matthew 12:8, Christian Standard Bible

I absolutely love Sunday. I love going to church, partaking of the sacrament, taking naps, playing games with family, and remembering my Savior's sacrifice for me. However, nothing can compare to how much the Pharisees loved the Sabbath. They were bananas about it. However, instead of making God the Lord of the Sabbath, they made laws and rules the lord of the Sabbath. Here is a list of a few things they didn't do:

> Sowing, plowing, reaping, binding sheaves, threshing, winnowing, selecting, grinding, sifting, kneading, baking . . . the making of two loops, weaving two threads, dividing two threads, tying and untying, sewing two stitches, tearing in order to sew two stitches . . . writing two letters, erasing in order to write two letters [over the erasure], building, tearing down, extinguishing, kindling, striking with a hammer, [and] carrying out from one domain to another.[384]

The Pharisees were serious about Sabbath day observance. One day on Shabbat, Jesus's disciples picked corn to eat and the Pharisees complained to Jesus saying, "Why are they breaking the law by harvesting grain on the Sabbath?"[385]

Whom Say Ye that I Am?

Jesus answered, "The Sabbath was made to meet the needs of people, and not people to meet the requirements of the Sabbath. So the Son of Man is Lord, even over the Sabbath!"[386]

Jesus was trying to teach the Pharisees that the Sabbath isn't a list of dos and don'ts. They were so focused on the rules that they missed the whole point of the Sabbath. Jesus called the Pharisees "whitewashed tombs—beautiful on the outside but filled on the inside with dead people's bones and all sorts of impurity."[387]

The Sabbath isn't rituals and rules. It's a relationship with Jesus. Jesus came to give us rest. The Sabbath is a gift of rest, peace, and renewal. When we are trying to earn our way to the celestial kingdom, we can't relax. Because of Jesus's sacrifice on the cross, we can forever cease laboring to earn the kingdom, resting in the grace of the Lord of the Sabbath, even as we labor to build it. "The kingdom is yours and the blessings thereof are yours, and the riches of eternity are yours."[388]

Jesus gave us the Sabbath as a day of healing, loving, and coming closer to Him. It is to remind us of His love for us and the rest we receive from Him. Jesus taught, "Keep the Sabbath, my day of rest, because it is a sign between you and me for all time to come, to show that I, the Lord, have made you my own people. You must keep the day of rest, because it is sacred . . . The people of Israel are to keep this day as a sign of the covenant. It is a permanent sign between the people of Israel and me."[389]

The Sabbath is a sign of our covenant marriage to Jesus. It is a sign that we are His. It is a sign of God's love for each one of us and His eternal and atoning sacrifice to save us. Jesus is our Sabbath rest.

The Pharisees and the proud focus on rules and rituals while the humble focus on their relationship with Jesus. The proud trust in what they can do for God while the humble trust in what Jesus has already done for them. The proud follow a list of rules and regulations to prove themselves worthy while the humble relax in Jesus's grace. The proud work to earn salvation while the humble rest in God's grace. The Sabbath is a joy and delight when we focus on our relationship with Jesus. It is a chore and a burden when we focus on a list of rules.

Jesus's name is Lord of the Sabbath. Your new name is **humble**. All those who recognize Jesus and humble themselves before Him will be exalted.[390]

Mitchell C. Taylor

Man of Sorrows

*He is despised and rejected of men; a man of
sorrows, and acquainted with grief.*
Isaiah 53:3, King James Version

When I first learned about this name, I was deeply confused. I asked myself, "How can Jesus be a man of sorrows?" God is love[391] and joy, not sadness and sorrow. We are created in the image of God, and we are that we "might have joy."[392]

The name 'Man of Sorrows' comes from Isaiah 53:3 which reads, "He is despised and rejected of men; a man of sorrows, and acquainted with grief: and we hid as it were our faces from him; he was despised, and we esteemed him not." The reason Isaiah used this name was not because Jesus was a sad, lonely man. It is because He experienced such great suffering that caused Him "the greatest of all, to tremble because of pain."[393] Jesus took upon Himself the whole world's sin, pain, sorrow, and sickness. He is a Man of Sorrows because of the sorrow He endured for us.

If you ever feel that nobody understands how you feel, you might be right, but Jesus always understands you. Jesus experienced everything you are feeling. He experienced your heartache, illness, mistake, and sadness. Jesus was the sin bearer for each one of us to ensure we can return into His loving arms.

Jesus could have focused on the pain, heartache, and sadness, but he didn't. He kept his focus on the joy of redeeming His lost sheep. You don't have to fear whether you will be good enough. Christ has already taken upon Himself the penalty of your sins. You have no need to worry. It is finished. Jesus has overcome. Jesus lives, and He is mighty to save![394] You don't have to be the man or woman of sorrows, because Jesus already is.

Jesus's name is Man of Sorrows. Your new name is **joyful**. Jesus declares, "Your sins are forgiven you; you are clean before me; therefore, lift up your heads and rejoice."[395] "Come and share your master's joy!"[396]

Whom Say Ye that I Am?

Master

Ye call me Master and Lord: and ye say well; for so I am.
John 13:13, King James Version

Jesus taught His apostles, "the greatest among you must become like a person of lower status and the leader like a servant."[397]

The apostles were probably like, "What? The greatest is the servant? How does that make sense?" While this paradox may be confusing, Jesus was the greatest example of the master being a servant. He exemplified this perfectly when He washed the apostles' feet. Even though Jesus is the Master, He filled a basin with water and washed the apostles' stinky, dirty feet—a task meant only for a servant.

During Jesus's earthly ministry, many recognized Him as a great teacher, but fewer recognized Him as their Master and Savior. When you make someone your master, you give your full heart and will to their command. Video games, television, and memes can all be great tools, but they also can become masters that lead to unwise decisions. We need to decide who or what will be our master.

Jesus desires that you follow Him with full purpose of heart. Jesus teaches, "No one can serve two masters; for either he will hate the one and love the other, or else he will be loyal to the one and despise the other. You cannot serve God and mammon."[398]

You can't be loyal to two opposing sides. "A man being a servant of the devil cannot follow Christ; and if he follow Christ he cannot be a servant of the devil."[399] It is impossible to serve two masters. "You must choose for yourselves today whom you will serve."[400]

Jesus is Master over all the elements, the animals, and the earth. He is the Master who is in control. Let's look to our Master, Jesus, and have His will become our will.

Jesus's name is Master. Your new name is **servant**. "I am the Lord your God, and . . . you [are] . . . my . . . servants."[401] Those who give their hearts to God and serve[402] will hear Jesus say, "Well done, you good and faithful servant. You have been faithful over a few things. I will make you ruler over many things. Enter the joy of your master."[403]

Mitchell C. Taylor

Mediator

*For there is one God, and one mediator, between
God and men, the man Jesus Christ.*
1 Timothy 2:5, King James Version

I used to get into plenty of fights with my siblings. My mom or dad would have to come and break it up. They would help us resolve the issue and forgive. In these situations, my parents acted as mediators.

A mediator is someone who helps opposing sides come to an agreement. They discuss until both parties are satisfied. Parents are mediators between siblings, and Jesus is a mediator between us and God.

Jesus's mediation is the only means whereby we can gain salvation. If we try to stand alone before the throne of God, we are doomed. Without Christ, "the wages of sin is death"[404] and we are unworthy to enter God's kingdom. We all sin and sin stands between us and God.

We can do nothing on our own to mediate for ourselves. No matter how persuasive our argument, how eloquent our rhetoric, or how good our deeds, the case is settled. Based on our merits, we are unable to return to our heavenly home, but there is hope.

"[Jesus] is to be mediator between God and man; between the offended sovereign and the offending sinner. If Jesus were only divine, he could not represent people. If Jesus were only human, he could not plead with God. Deity alone was too high for human beings; humanity alone was too low for God. Jesus must be both at once and so be the middle person touching both God and human beings."[405]

When all appears lost, Jesus comes bursting in and tells the law, "Come now, let us settle the matter."[406] He tells justice how He "rescued us from the curse pronounced by the law. [That] when he was hung on the cross, he took upon himself the curse for our wrongdoing."[407] He tells the law how He "[bled] at every pore, and . . . suffer[ed] both body and spirit"[408] on our behalf.

After Jesus tells the law how He "takes away the sin of the world,"[409] the law and Jesus shake hands, and you become "perfect in Christ"[410] no longer "under *the* Law, but under grace."[411] The law has no more hold upon you. You declare like Paul, "I no longer live. Christ lives in me . . .

Whom Say Ye that I Am?

I live by putting my trust in the Son of God. He was the One Who loved me and gave Himself for me."[412]

When we tie our worthiness and worth to our own performance, it leads to feelings of anxiety, depression, and shame. Martin Luther, one of the great and courageous forerunners of the Restoration, declared, "The more someone tries to bring peace to his conscience through his own righteousness, the more disquieted he makes it."[413]

The more we understand Jesus's roll as our mediator and experience His grace, the greater our "freedom from shame and the associated depression, anxiety, and perfectionism."[414]

Jesus came to relieve us from the shame of sin. Jesus came to remove our feelings of worry, anxiety, and distress. Our Mediator has satisfied the law, and we are declared worthy in His sight. We are perfect in Christ.[415]

"Christ came with this new agreement so that all who are invited may come and have forever all the wonders God has promised them. For Christ died to rescue them from the penalty of the sins they had committed."[416] Christ has paid the price and invites all to come unto Him.

Jesus's name is Mediator. Your new name is **relieved**. "God [is your] defender! When [you were] in trouble, [Christ] helped [you]"[417] and set you free from sin.

Meek and Lowly

I am meek and lowly in heart.
Matthew 11:29, King James Version

In our world today it can be extremely difficult to be meek and lowly. People are constantly yelling at each other, Karens are bickering about every little thing, and there are feelings of hate and entitlement. While our world is far from perfect, we can look to Jesus for how to be more meek and lowly.

When I first heard meek and lowly, I thought, "That sounds awful. Being meek makes you a target for bullying. And being lowly . . . who would want that?" But now I know my first thoughts were far from the truth and being meek and lowly is an amazing thing. To get a greater understanding of the name 'Meek and Lowly', we will separate it into its two different parts.

When someone is meek, they are patient, gentle, and long-suffering. The perfect example of meekness is, of course, Jesus. Instead of forcing us to choose Him, He is patient and beckons us to come.

When we sin, Jesus doesn't condemn us or get angry. He holds us even closer so we can feel His exquisite love. He will never send us away. He wants to be with us so much He was willing to bear our sins and be nailed to a cross. Even while in excruciating pain, from the cross, He declared, "Father, forgive them, because they do not know what they are doing."[418]

Jesus was so patient that He didn't condemn the very people who killed Him. He quickly forgave them. Jesus is never your enemy. He will always accept you no matter what you have done, even if you crucify Him! Jesus is meek and eager to receive all! Jesus will not exclude you.

Being lowly can be described as viewing yourself as less than the dust of the earth.[419] Two of the synonyms for lowly are humble and submissive.

Jesus never sought to do His own will. He told His disciples, "I don't try to please myself, but I try to please the One who sent me."[420] He was so humble that He suffered for each one of us. He could've stopped the pain at any time, but instead He uttered the words, "not my will, but yours, be done."[421]

Jesus is a king, but during His earthly ministry, He didn't appear as a king. He didn't want to appear superior. With an earthly king, only a few privileged are called to come before him. With Jesus, He invites all to come to Him. He abased Himself so He could draw near to us—a bunch of sinners. Even though He was the Son of God, He didn't see Himself as greater than anyone else. Jesus taught, "Whoever makes himself great will be humbled, and whoever humbles himself will be made great."[422]

While the proud exclude and demean, the humble lift and inspire. Jesus takes the outcast and the filthy, and makes them His friends. He receives us sinners and eats with us.

The Pharisees and some in our day think they are better than others because of the knowledge they have or the church they affiliate with. "It was said of an old Greek philosopher, that he wrote over his door, 'No one except the learned may enter here.'"[423] Jesus on the contrary writes, "All may enter and be saved."

Become meek and lowly like the Meek and Lowly One and "acknowledge your unworthiness before God at all times."[424] "Apart from Jesus, there is no such thing as a 'good person.' There is no distinction between righteous and unrighteous . . . Without the grace of Jesus, there is only one category: sinner."[425] Let's be humble like Jesus and declare our dependence on Him. "All those . . . who humble themselves will be exalted."[426]

Jesus's name is Meek and Lowly. Your new name is **exalted**. "God blesses those who are poor and realize their need for him, for the kingdom of heaven is theirs."[427]

The Mighty God

And he shall be called . . . The Mighty God.
Isaiah 9:6, King James Version

During Jesus's earthly ministry, "He went about doing good . . . [and did] many mighty miracles."[428] Jesus performed so many great and mighty miracles that "if they were all written down . . . the whole world could not hold the books that would be written."[429]

The word 'mighty' is translated from the word *globor*, which means champion or strength. 'God' in Hebrew is the word *El*, which means unmeasurable strength. Jesus is the champion with unmeasurable strength. There is nothing that Jesus can't do. Who would want to fight against Him and His people?

While Jesus is our Mighty Champion, some trust in the "arm of flesh."[430] They trust in their own abilities and strength instead of Jesus's unmeasurable strength.

Our might, apart from God, is translated from the word *gibbor* while God's strength is translated from the word *abir*. As to our own might, we are "less than the dust of the earth . . . [and] can do nothing without [Jesus]."[431] When we are in Christ, there is absolutely nothing that can't be done. Let go of the *gibbor* of men and start trusting in the *abir* of God.

Jesus is The Mighty God, our Unmeasurable Champion. When He is on our side, "all things are possible."[432] He is our God who is "mighty to save,"[433] and through His power we will overcome sin and death.

Jesus's name is The Mighty God. Your new name is **unbeatable**. When you recognize you are weak,[434] you will "be strong in the Lord, relying on his mighty strength."[435] "The LORD your God is with you. He is a hero who saves you. He happily rejoices over you, renews you with his love, and celebrates over you with shouts of joy."[436] In Christ you are unbeatable.

Omnipotent

I know that you can do anything, and no one can stop you.
Job 42:2, New Living Translation

God's omnipotence is seen in the creation. He said, "Let there be," and it was so.[437] What Jesus commands is brought to pass. Jesus is all-powerful, all-knowing, and infinite. "What God says will always come true."[438]

Jesus's omnipotence is also seen during His earthy ministry. The Gospel of Matthew records, "Large crowds came and brought many people who were paralyzed or blind or lame or unable to talk. They placed them, and many others, in front of Jesus, and he healed them all. Everyone was amazed at what they saw and heard. People who had never spoken could now speak. The lame were healed, the paralyzed could walk, and the blind were able to see. Everyone was praising the God of Israel."[439]

When we say Jesus is omnipotent, it means He has all power. "For nothing . . . is too hard for the Lord."[440] He has unlimited power. Even though we call Jesus omnipotent, I don't think we believe it. We like to confine Him into a tiny box of finite power. We lock Him in this box with the key of works when we try to rely on the "arm of flesh."[441] We believe we can do it by ourselves and wonder why we are so discouraged and depressed. We forget what Jesus teaches in John 15:5 that "you can do nothing without me."[442] We rely on our works and try to do it on our own, but "whosoever shall exalt himself shall be abased."[443]

We go through life trusting in our abilities and power while we should be relying on Jesus's might, mind, and strength.[444] We think when something great happens it's because of our great work and effort to bring it to pass. We forget whose hands made it possible. Without Christ "you are nothing but a windbag."[445] We are "less than the dust of the earth"[446] and must be "awakened . . . to [our] nothingness . . . and [our] worthless, and fallen state."[447]

We must accept the humble pie and recognize our "unworthiness before God at all times."[448] We must see that we have no power to accomplish anything and are useless without Jesus. Once we realize our nothingness before God, we can be effective instruments in His hands.

King Mosiah taught his people, "I would that ye should remember, and always retain in remembrance, the greatness of God, and your own nothingness, and his goodness and long-suffering toward you, unworthy creatures, and humble yourselves even in the depths of humility, calling on the name of the Lord daily."[449] You must "never forget that apart from Christ and God's grace you are an unworthy, guilty, creature."[450] You must remember Jesus is all-powerful, but on your own you are a powerless servant.

Even though Jesus has all power, sometimes we fear because we are finite and limited in our abilities. We feel weak, but Jesus makes "weak things become strong."[451] Through His strength we are made strong. Jesus has no limits. God is all-powerful and nothing is more powerful than Him, not even sin and death can conquer Him. In Jesus, "nothing is impossible."[452] You "can do all things through Christ."[453]

Jesus's name is Omnipotent. Your new name is **unlimited**. "[Jesus's] grace is all you need. [Your] power works best in weakness. So now [you are] glad to boast about [your] weaknesses, so that the power of Christ can work through [you]."[454]

One

And the L*ORD* *shall be king over all the earth: in that day shall there be one* L*ORD*, *and his name one.*
Zechariah 14:9, King James Version

John 1:14 declares of Jesus, "We have seen his glory, the glory of the one and only Son, who came from the Father, full of grace and truth."[455] Jesus came to earth to unite us with our Heavenly Father.

Jesus declares in John 17:21–22, "That they all may be one; as thou, Father, art in me, and I in thee, that they also may be one in us: that the world may believe that thou hast sent me. And the glory which thou gavest me I have given them; that they may be one, even as we are one."[456]

Because Jesus is One with the Father, He can declare, "Everything the Father has is mine."[457] Jesus wants us to become one with Him so we can receive everything the Father has.

When we are born again, we become one with Jesus through the covenant of baptism. Baptism is like a marriage. Jesus teaches that when a man and a woman get married "the two will become one flesh. So they are no longer two, but one."[458]

When a man and a woman get married, they are to become one in purpose. They work together to raise and teach their family. This is the same with Heavenly Father and Jesus. They are one in purpose.

The Hebrew word translated into 'one' is *ehhad,* which means unity. Jeff A. Benner taught, "While this word is often translated as 'one,' where the actual Hebraism is lost, it is better translated as a 'unity.'"[459] When you see the word 'one' in the Bible, you can replace it with the word 'unified.'

God the Eternal Father and Jesus are one in purpose and function. Their purpose is found in Moses 1:39, "For behold, this is my work and my glory—to bring to pass the immortality and eternal life of man." When we become one with Jesus, we join Heavenly Father and Jesus in this eternal mission.

Jesus's name is One. Your new name is **unified**. Jesus's purpose and mission become your purpose and mission. His words become your words. "God will give you the right words at the right time."[460] His ways become your ways, and "God will supply all your needs according to his riches."[461] All the riches of Heavenly Father are yours!

Our Passover

For even Christ our Passover is sacrificed for us.
1 Corinthians 5:7, King James Version

In Jewish culture, the Passover is the time they remember their deliverance from the Egyptians by the Lord. Moses commanded Pharaoh to "Let my people go"[462] but Pharaoh didn't. So the Lord sent frogs to infest the land.⁴⁶³ He sent "lice throughout all the land of Egypt"⁴⁶⁴ He even caused fire and hail to rain on the land of Egypt.⁴⁶⁵ But Pharaoh didn't free the children of Israel.

The Lord told Moses, "I will pass through the land of Egypt and strike down every firstborn son . . . in the land of Egypt."⁴⁶⁶ There is only one way to survive this destroying angel. The Lord commanded them to put blood on their doors to "distinguish them . . . And when I see the blood, I will pass over you, and no plague will befall you to destroy you, when I strike the land of Egypt."⁴⁶⁷

When the appointed day arrived, all the firstborn in the land of Egypt were killed if they didn't have the blood on their door. Since the children of Israel listened to the commands of the Lord, they were spared. The destroying angel passed over the children of Israel who had the mark of the Lamb's blood on their door.

Likewise, because of Jesus's redeeming blood, the destroying angel of sin and death passes over us. The destroying angel doesn't pass over us because we are worthy or have good works. The angel of death passes over because of whose blood was spilled for us.

We all have sinned and the punishment hovers over each one of us. We deserve a life of endless torment, but we are spared because of Jesus's willingness to spill His blood for us all. Jesus's blood protects us from the penalty of sin and death.

The consequences of sin and death can pass over us because Jesus has bought us with His blood and are our "garments [are] washed white through the blood of the Lamb."⁴⁶⁸ Jesus has made us clean and worthy so the destroying angel can pass over.

The Passover isn't just an event to remember that God had mercy on the children of Israel. It's a time to remember Jesus's great atoning sacrifice for us all. If we are with Jesus, the angel of sin and death will pass over us because we are perfect in the "blood of the Lamb."⁴⁶⁹

Jesus's name is Our Passover. Your new name is **spared**. Jesus has forgiven our transgressions, put our sins out of sight,⁴⁷⁰ and declares to the Father, ". . . spare these my brethren that believe on my name, that they may come unto me and have everlasting life."⁴⁷¹

Mitchell C. Taylor

Perfection

By the grace of God ye are perfect in Christ.
Moroni 10:32

Elder Jeffrey R. Holland closed his talk, "Be Ye Therefore Perfect—Eventually" saying, "I do so in the very name of Perfection itself, of Him who has never been clumsy or inadequate but who loves all of us who are, even the Lord Jesus Christ, amen."[472] Elder Holland called Jesus "Perfection," for that is one of His names.

Matthew 5:48 records Jesus saying during the sermon on the mount, "Be ye therefore perfect, even as your Father which is in heaven is perfect."[473] The English dictionary defines perfect as "completely free from faults or defect; as good as it is possible to be; flawless."

With this English definition, it may appear that Jesus is demanding a sinless performance. This misunderstanding can lead to perfectionism, which is defined as a tendency to demand of oneself a flawless level of performance. Perfectionism leads to depression, anxiety, feeling of self-loathing, worthlessness, shame, fear of God, and other mental health problems.[474]

To correctly understand Jesus's directive "Be ye therefore perfect," we need to look at the Greek word *teleios*, which is translated to 'perfect' in the King James Version. *Teleios* comes from the word *telos*, which means goal or purpose. *Teleios* means to complete your goal or purpose. Using this Greek meaning of the word *teleios*, Jesus is saying, "Complete the goal of your creation. Fulfill your purpose/mission."

This verse could read, "Complete your purpose/mission, even as your Father, which is in heaven, has completed his mission/purpose." God has told us our purpose saying, "Men [and women] are, that they might have joy."[475] We fulfill the purpose of our creation when we are joyful. God wants us to be happy! With this definition of our purpose, we could understand Jesus's directive as, "Be ye therefore happy, even as your Father, which is in heaven, is happy."

The Greek word *teleios* should not be confused with *anamartetos*, which means "without sin or sinless."[476] The Greek word *anamartetos* is used in John chapter 8. The scribes and Pharisees brought a woman taken in adultery to Jesus and asked, "Moses in the law commanded us, that such should be stoned: but what sayest thou?"[477] Jesus answered, "He that is without sin among you, let him first cast a stone at her."[478] The words "He that is without sin" are the English translation of the Greek word *anamartetos*. The Greek word *anamartetos* could also be translated to the English word "perfect" to mean one who is flawless or completely free of sin. This verse could be translated as "He who is perfect, let him first cast a stone at her." Both Greek words *teleios* (reaching one's goal) and *anamartetos* (without sin or sinless) can be translated to the same English word "perfect" but their meanings are very, very different. In the Sermon on the Mount, Jesus is not commanding us to be without sin or sinless.

Jesus is the only sinless person and is the only person who could be said to be perfect with both the definition of *teleios* (reaching one's goal) and *anamartetos* (without sin or sinless). Jesus is perfect not just because He lived a sinless life but also because He completes His purpose/mission as the Savior and Redeemer of the world perfectly.[479]

Nephi writes of Jesus saying, "He doeth not anything save it be for the benefit of the world; for he loveth the world, even that he layeth down his own life that he may draw all men unto him. Wherefore, he commandeth none that they shall not partake of his salvation."[480] Jesus saves people perfectly.

We can have complete trust and confidence in Jesus to save us because we know He is a perfect Savior. Jesus will always do His job. He is perfect in His role as Savior, Redeemer, and Forgiver of Sins. He perfectly fulfills His purpose to bring to pass the immortality and eternal life of man.[481]

Jesus didn't intend the statement "Be ye therefore perfect" to be used as a verbal hammer to beat us up over our sins and shortcomings.[482] Jesus's perfection (sinlessness) isn't a sign to show us we suck or we aren't good enough, but rather it is a sign of Jesus's power to save us.

Elder Holland declared, "Our only hope for true perfection is in receiving it as a gift from heaven—we can't 'earn' it."[483]

Perfection is not something we do or earn. It's a gift we receive. The prophet Moroni taught us how to be perfect (sinless). He said, "Yea, come unto Christ, and be perfected in him."[484] We become perfect in

Jesus despite our sins and shortcomings. The only way to achieve perfection (be without sin) is to become one with Jesus, the only Perfect One.

Jesus's name is Perfection. Your new name is **perfect**. You are declared perfect, not because you are sinless but because you are one with Jesus and He is sinless. Romans 8:1 declares the good news that even though you are full of sins and shortcomings, "There is . . . no condemnation to those who are in Christ Jesus."[485]

Physician

Jesus went about . . . healing all manner of sickness and all manner of disease among the people.
Matthew 4:23, King James Version

Mark 5 shares a story of a woman dealing with great pain and sickness for twelve years. "She had borne much agony under the care of many physicians and had spent all she had, but to no avail. Instead, her condition had only grown worse."[486]

She searched tirelessly for a cure. She went to doctor after doctor but found no help or healing. Bankrupt, heartbroken, and hopeless, this woman could have easily given up, but she pressed forward. When she heard about Jesus, hope ignited within her. She heard that Jesus gave sight to the blind, hearing to the deaf, and even raised the dead. These stories built her faith, and she believed Jesus could heal her.

Her opportunity to see Jesus came while He was on His way to heal Jairus's daughter. However, a very large crowd surrounded Jesus, and He didn't seem accessible. She thought, "If I can just touch his robe, I will be healed."[487] She pushed through the crowd, desperately trying to get close enough to touch Jesus. "As soon as she touched [his robe], her bleeding stopped, and she knew she was healed."[488]

"Jesus realized at once that healing power had gone out from him, so he turned around in the crowd and asked, 'Who touched my robe?' . . . The frightened woman, trembling at the realization of what had happened to her, came and fell to her knees in front of [Jesus] and told him what she had done. And [Jesus] said to her, 'Daughter, your faith has made you well. Go in peace. Your suffering is over.'"[489]

Whom Say Ye that I Am?

Like this woman, we are all sick. We all are infected with sin with no cure. There is only one way to be healed of this awful sickness. We need to go to Jesus, who has "healing in his wings."[490] He wants to cure you.

Not everyone recognizes they are sick and need the great Physician to heal them. The Pharisees were sick with sin but claimed they were righteous. Jesus said to them, "It is not those who are well who need a doctor, but those who are sick . . . For I have come to call not those who think they are righteous, but those who know they are sinners."[491]

Imagine you are at the doctor's office, and he tells you, "I am sorry. You have cancer."

You reply, "No I don't. I'm healthy. You don't know my body."

The doctor shows you the test results, "Look, you have cancer. Please let me help you."

You confidently reply, "I don't have cancer, and I don't need your help."

Doctors can't help someone who doesn't think they need help. C. S. Lewis wrote, "Christianity tells people to repent and promises them forgiveness. It therefore has nothing (as far as I know) to say to people who do not know they have done anything to repent of and who do not feel that they need any forgiveness. It is after you have realized that there is a real Moral Law, and a Power behind the law, and that you have broken that law and put yourself wrong with that Power—it is after all this, and not a moment sooner, that Christianity begins to talk. When you know you are sick, you will listen to the doctor."[492]

Romans 3:10 reads, "There is none that are righteous no not one."[493] We are all infected with sin, but do we recognize our need for the Physician? If you don't believe you're sick, Jesus can't help you. You'll be like the Pharisees who were in desperate need of a cure but oblivious they were sick.

Let's be like the woman with an issue of blood and recognize our sickness and need for a cure. Come to Jesus sick, broken, and unclean, and let Him heal you.

This woman spent twelve years searching for a cure, but she never found one. When she went to Jesus, she was healed immediately. We all are sick and need a Master Healer. You can go from source to source looking for a cure to sin. You can go to all the doctors, but none will be able to heal you. You can't heal yourself. But if you turn to Jesus, the Mighty Physician, you will be healed. Dr. Jesus is able heal all your sins.

Jesus's name is Physician. Your new name is **healed**. When you come to Jesus begging, "Have mercy on me, O Lord . . . heal me,"[494] the great Physician enthusiastically proclaims, "Be healed!"[495] "Whatever Jesus lays his hands upon lives."[496]

Potter

O Lord, thou art our father; we are the clay, and thou
our potter; and we all are the work of thy hand.
Isaiah 64:8, King James Version

I'm not a very artistic person. Anything I try to create usually ends up in the trash. Jesus on the other hand is a perfect artist. He molds us into works of beauty and splendor.

Creating a pot is a slow process of changing, reforming, and refining. Likewise, Jesus slowly shapes and refines us over an eternity. There's no quick way to become like Jesus. It's a long process.

Without the hands of the potter, the clay remains unchanged. Can a piece of clay form itself into a pot? Of course not. Likewise, we can't become like Jesus on our own. We need the hands of Jesus to transform and refine us. Jesus gives us shape, purpose, and meaning.

When we allow Jesus to put us on His potter wheel, we become more than we ever imagined possible. Alone we remain an unchanged piece of clay. In the hands of Jesus, we become a priceless piece of art.

Let the Master Potter take a hold of you and lead you to become the person He wants you to be. He knows what is best for you. Let Him be in control.

Jesus's name is Potter. Your new name is **transformed**. Jesus makes "weak things become strong."[497] His hands will never let you go, and "no man is able to pluck [you] out [of His hands]."[498] He "transform[s] our lowly body to be like his glorious body."[499] Jesus will transform you into a masterpiece.

Whom Say Ye that I Am?

The Prince of Peace

. . . and he shall be called . . . The Prince of Peace.
Isaiah 9:6, King James Version

The word 'prince' in the Bible is translated from the Hebrew word *sar*, which means in charge or leader. The word "peace" is translated from the word *shalom*, which means perfect rest. Jesus doesn't give us ordinary peace. He gives us *perfect* peace and rest.

After a long day of teaching, Jesus and the apostles "dismissed the crowd"[500] and climbed into a boat. While they were sailing, "a storm struck the lake. Waves started splashing into the boat, and it was about to sink."[501] Desperately, the apostles started doing everything in their power to save the boat—lowering the sail, holding fast to the tiller, and bailing water. While the apostles were yelling to communicate with each another, Jesus "was in the stern, asleep on a pillow."[502]

The apostles, with all their energy depleted, awoke Jesus and said, "Master . . . don't you care that we're going to die?"[503] Jesus got up and "rebuked the wind, and said to the sea, 'Peace. Be still.' And the wind ceased, and there was a great calm."[504]

Everybody wants to have peace, but we are usually like the apostles frantically screaming and running around in terror trying to survive. There is only one answer to the question, "Where can I turn for peace?"[505] Jesus!

When Jesus, The Prince of Peace, is in our boat, it will not sink. However, when the storms hit, it is easy to forget who is in our boat and be filled with anxiety, fear, and worry as were the apostles. We must remember that Jesus is in our boat and "the storm cannot penetrate [us]."[506]

When Jesus says the words, "Peace. Be still," He isn't only commanding the waves; He is also inviting us to be still and find rest. We need to stop trying to save the boat on our own. Let go of the tiller, and the sail, and let Jesus guide you to celestial shores. We will never find peace in our abilities. We must turn to The Prince of Peace, who gives us rest and a "peace . . . which transcends all understanding."[507]

A synonym for peace is reconciliation. Jesus paid the price of our sins so we can be reconciled. When we understand Jesus's character and our relationship with Him, we are filled with peace for He has saved us. When we are with The Prince of Peace, we have no need to worry, because no storm is mightier than our God!

Jesus's name is The Prince of Peace. Your new name is **peaceful**. Jesus "is [your] peace."[508] Jesus says to you, "In me you may have peace. In the world you will have trouble. But take heart! I have overcome the world!"[509] Jesus is "the path of peace."[510]

Prophet

The LORD thy God will raise up unto thee a Prophet from the midst of thee, of thy brethren, like unto me, unto him ye shall harken.
Deuteronomy 18:15, King James Version

In Deuteronomy 18:15, God promised He would raise a Prophet to lead and guide them. The Jews were earnestly looking for this prophesied prophet when they asked John the Baptist, "Are you the Prophet we are expecting?"[511]

John answered them saying, "No . . . I am not the Messiah."[512]

John the Baptist was a prophet, but not the Prophet who was also the Messiah, Savior, and Redeemer.

The people then asked John, "Then who are you?"[513]

John answered, "I am the voice that cries in the wilderness: 'Prepare the way of THE LORD JEHOVAH.'"[514]

"The next day John seeth Jesus coming unto him and saith, Behold the Lamb of God, which taketh away the sin of the world!"[515]

John's role as a prophet was to lead people to Jesus, the Prophet, the Messiah, and the Redeemer. He said, "I came . . . that [Jesus] might be revealed to Israel."[516] "I . . . testified that [Jesus] is the Son of God."[517]

All prophets throughout history have the same goal—to help people come to Jesus. So why is Jesus a Prophet? Jesus's role as a Prophet is to lead us to Heavenly Father.

In John 14, Jesus tells His apostles, "In my Father's house are many rooms. If it were not so, would I have told you that I am going to prepare a place for you? If I go away and prepare a place for you, I will come again and take you to myself, so that where I am you may be also. You know the way to where I am going."[518]

Thomas, a little confused, said "Lord . . . we do not know where You are going, so how can we know the way?"[519] Jesus answered Thomas, "I am the way, the truth, and the life. No one can come to the Father except through me."[520]

The King James Version of John 14:2 reads, "In my Father's house are many mansions." A more accurate translation of this verse is: "In my Father's house are many rooms."[521] Jesus is trying to paint a clear picture of where we are going. Jesus is going to live with His Father, and He is preparing a room for us to join Him. We will not have a mansion down the street or in the same city. We have a room waiting for us in Heavenly Father's home. Jesus has promised, "I go and prepare a place for you . . . Where I am, there you may be also."[522] Follow the Prophet, Jesus. He is the way to our Heavenly Father's house.

Jesus's name is Prophet. Your new name is **watched over**. Jesus has prepared a room for you in Heavenly Father's house. Jesus is the "watchman upon the tower."[523] He will protect you "from the hands of the destroyer."[524] Jesus will make certain you arrive safely to your heavenly home. You can count on Jesus's promise. You "will live in the house of the LORD forever."[525]

Rabbi and Rabboni

Rabbi, thou art the Son of God; thou art the King of Israel.[526]
—Nathanael (John 1:49, King James Version)

During His earthly ministry, Jesus did a lot of teaching. He taught in the streets, mountains, and synagogues. He taught anywhere and anyone. Even as a teenager, He taught in the temple and the people were "astonished at his understanding."[527] Nicodemus, a ruler of the Jews, recognized Jesus as a teacher come from God.[528] Everyone who encountered Jesus testified He was an outstanding teacher.

In Jewish culture, you learned the scriptures and the Torah from a rabbi. Jesus had a great understanding of the scriptures and Torah, but He didn't learn from a rabbi. This confused people because Jesus's earthly father was a carpenter. The people questioned, "Is not this Joseph's son?"[529]

Luke 4 records Jesus teaching from Isaiah 61 at synagogue. This chapter prophesies about the coming Messiah and the miracles that He would do. After Jesus finished teaching, He closed the scrolls and declared, "This day is the scripture fulfilled in your ears."[530]

Jesus is much more than a great teacher and rabbi. He is the Messiah who came to redeem us all. The Pharisees saw Jesus's claim as blasphemy while others recognized Him as their Savior and the promised Messiah.

Another title similar to rabbi is rabboni. This title means "my master" and is one of the most honorable titles you could receive. In all recorded scripture, Jesus is only called Rabboni once by Mary Magdalene after His resurrection.

On Sunday morning, Mary went to the Tomb to anoint Jesus with oil. When she reached the tomb, she saw the stone rolled away and began to cry.

Jesus appeared outside the tomb, but Mary didn't recognize Him. When Jesus called her by name saying, "Mary!"[531] She "turned to him and cried out, 'Rabboni!'"[532]

Mary probably used this title frequently for the man who rescued her from seven devils.[533] Mary was a true believer who accompanied Jesus in life, death, and resurrection. She was with Him as He hung on the cross,[534] and as He laid in the tomb.[535] Mary was the first person to be with Jesus following His resurrection. Mary greeted Jesus with the biggest hug you could ever imagine. She embraced Him for so long, that He had to kindly ask her to let go saying, "Do not hold on to me, for I have not yet ascended to the Father."[536]

Mary recognized Jesus as much more than a teacher. She knew Him as the Christ, her Rabboni (Master), and best friend.

Jesus's name is Rabbi and Rabboni. Your new name is **believer**. "If you openly declare that Jesus is Lord and believe in your heart that God raised him from the dead,"[537] you are a "true believer."[538]

Whom Say Ye that I Am?

Redeemer

I know that thou are redeemed, because of the righteousness of thy redeemer.
2 Nephi 2:3

Our Heavenly Father sent Jesus to "redeem mankind from their sins."[539] Redeem means to compensate for the faults of someone else or to gain or regain possession of something in exchange for payment. Jesus paid the price for our redemption by bleeding from every pore in Gethsemane and suffering crucifixion on Calvary.

When Jesus redeemed us, He freed us from the captivity, blame, and debt of sin. Jesus's mission is to reclaim the lost. Jesus loves us so much that "[He] gave himself for us, that he might redeem us from all iniquity."[540] It doesn't say Jesus redeemed us of some iniquity or a lot of iniquity. It says He redeemed us from *all* iniquity.

In order to be saved, we must be clean of all sin or be what is called justified. What does it mean to be justified? "To be justified is to be reconciled to God, pardoned from punishment for sin, and declared righteous and guiltless."[541] We can achieve justification in two ways—through the law or by Jesus.

To be justified by the law, we must keep all the laws all the time. We can't mess up even once because at the moment we commit a single sin, we become guilty and unclean and can no longer be justified or saved by the law. The apostle James taught, "For whosoever shall keep the whole law, and yet offend in one point, he is guilty of all."[542] There has been and only will be one person who keeps all the laws all the time and that person is Jesus.

Hoping to be justified by the law is a path that only leads to discouragement and hopelessness because it's an impossible task. The apostle Paul teaches, "For no one will ever be made right with God by obeying the law."[543] Lehi echoes these words in the Book of Mormon saying, "By the law no flesh is justified; or, by the law men are cut off. Yea, by the temporal law they were cut off; and also, by the spiritual law they perish from that which is good, and become miserable forever."[544]

Since salvation and justification by the law is impossible, Lehi continues his teaching by declaring the only way to be saved. He writes,

"Wherefore, redemption cometh in and through the Holy Messiah; for he is full of grace and truth. Behold, he offereth himself a sacrifice for sin, to answer the ends of the law, unto all those who have a broken heart and a contrite spirit; and unto none else can the ends of the law be answered. Wherefore, how great the importance to make these things known unto the inhabitants of the earth, that they may know that there is no flesh that can dwell in the presence of God, save it be through the merits, and mercy, and grace of the Holy Messiah . . . and they that believe in him shall be saved."[545]

Lehi testifies that all those with a broken heart and a contrite spirit who believe in Jesus will be saved in the celestial kingdom. When you become one with Jesus, He justifies you. He declares you righteous and guiltless even though you are a sinner and far from perfect.

Redemption doesn't come by your good works. Neither is it found in your religious devotion or by doing your best. "Redemption cometh in and through the Holy Messiah."[546] "Thou art redeemed, because of the righteousness of thy Redeemer."[547] Jesus declares you perfect in Christ and helps you become perfect like Him.

We didn't suffer and bleed from every pore. We weren't nailed to the cross. We weren't scourged and mocked. Jesus trod the winepress alone. It is finished. Jesus has reclaimed us to His possession. We are His. Jesus has told us, "Fear not, little children, for you are mine, and I have overcome the world."[548] He gave his life to pay our debt. Through Jesus, who is righteous, good, and perfect, we are saved. He purged *all* iniquity. The debt has been paid.

Even though Jesus has redeemed us, we still feel we must do our part. What is our part? Our part is to accept His gift. The way to be saved is simple. You believe in Jesus, you enter a relationship with Him, and you are forgiven of all your sins. Your debt becomes zero!

You don't have to earn your ticket into heaven. We aren't saved after all we can do. Jesus has already paid the price and is holding the ticket before you. You just have to accept His gift. We are only saved through the precious spilled blood of Jesus. Elder Jeffrey R. Holland taught in General Conference, "Our only hope for true perfection is in receiving it as a gift from heaven—we can't 'earn' it. Thus, the grace of Christ offers us . . . salvation from sorrow and sin and death."[549]

Whom Say Ye that I Am?

By calling Jesus our Redeemer, we confess that we cannot free ourselves from the bondage of sin and death. We confess that we are sick and need a physician to heal us. Jesus has dealt with sin once and for all! Through Jesus, we are made right with God. We are justified, perfect in Christ, not because we did anything, but because Jesus did everything. He is our Redeemer.

Jesus's name is Redeemer. Your new name is **redeemed**. Jesus gives you this promise, "I have blotted out your transgressions . . . I have redeemed you."[550] You can exclaim as did Nephi, "I glory in my Jesus, for he has redeemed my soul from hell."[551] Jesus is full of grace and truth.

Rest

Come to Me, all who are weary and burdened, and I will give you rest.
Matthew 11:28, New American Standard Bible

I don't like sleeping in. I get up at the crack of dawn. Many of my friends stay up late and pull all-nighters while I go to bed early and wake up at 5:30 a.m. No matter what your sleep pattern is, you need rest. Without it you will die. Your body will slowly waste away until you doze off and never wake up again. Just kidding. I have no idea how that works, but I do know rest is critical.

In our crazy, busy lives we don't want to rest. We may feel if we stop working, we are failures. Rest is radical and often counter to western culture, and yet Jesus wants us to rest. Jesus teaches, "Come to Me, all who are weary and burdened, and I will give you rest. Take My yoke upon you and learn from Me, for I am gentle and humble in heart, and you will find rest for your souls."[552] "For my yoke is easy and my burden is light."[553]

When you first read this, you might think, *A yoke? That doesn't sound restful. That sounds like more work.* I felt the same way until I learned something about oxen. In a yoke, two oxen are pulling a plow. While you might think these two oxen pull together, they actually don't. "It was common to place two oxen in the yoke when pulling a plow. An older, more experienced ox was matched with a younger inexperienced one so the younger would learn the task of plowing from the older."[554]

Jesus says, "Take My yoke upon you and learn of me." We are to learn from Him. We are the young, frail, inexperienced ox who needs help. Jesus is the older, experienced ox who carries the whole load. We are yoked with Christ, but we are only walking beside Him, gaining experience, while Jesus carries the whole load. Doesn't that sound much more restful? When Jesus says, "My yoke is easy," He isn't lying. He carries the whole load.

Some of us resist Jesus's invitation to carry our load. We want to carry the load ourselves. We work and work but make no progress. We fear we aren't good enough and will never make it.

In order to find rest in Christ, you need to stop trying hard to save yourself. You are trying to carry an impossible load. You need to let Christ take the load. He has already paid the price so you can rest. Enter His yoke and receive "the rest of the Lord."[555]

Jesus's name is Rest. Your new name is **serene**. Jesus has promised, "Your salvation requires you to turn back to me and stop your silly efforts to save yourselves. Your strength will come from settling down in complete dependence on me."[556] Jesus's yoke is easy. When you enter His yoke, you can rest.

The Resurrection and the Life

I am the resurrection, and the life: he that believeth in me, though he were dead, yet shall he live.[557]
—Jesus (John 11:25, King James Version)

During His time on earth, Jesus made a multitude of friends. Three of these friends were Mary, Martha, and Lazarus. The Bible records that "Jesus loved Martha, Mary, and Lazarus."[558] One day Lazarus became extremely ill, and Mary and Martha asked Jesus to come to their home in Bethany to heal him, but Lazarus died before Jesus arrived.

Prior to leaving for Bethany, Jesus told His disciples, "Our friend Lazarus has fallen asleep, but now I will go and wake him up."[559] Death to Jesus is just sleep.

Whom Say Ye that I Am?

When Jesus arrived in Bethany, Lazarus had been dead four days. In Jewish culture, it was believed that the spirit of the deceased lingered by the body for two days, but after the third day it was gone. So Lazarus wasn't just dead. He was dead, dead.

When Martha heard that Jesus was coming, she mete him outside the town and cried, "If you had been here, Lord, my brother would not have died!"[560]

Jesus comforted her saying, "Thy brother will rise again . . . I am the resurrection, and the life: he that believeth in me, though he were dead, yet shall he live."[561]

Jesus asked to be taken to the burial place of Lazarus. As they stood outside the tomb, Jesus shouted, "Lazarus, come out!"[562] Lazarus obeyed and exited his tomb still wrapped in his burial clothes. Jesus raised Lazarus from the dead. After seeing this mighty miracle, many believed in Jesus and "put their faith in him."[563]

When Jesus told Martha that Lazarus would live again, she responded, "I know that he will rise again in the resurrection at the last day."[564] Martha believed and viewed the resurrection as a future event, but Jesus showed her, and each of us, that the resurrection is a present reality. When we are in a personal relationship with Jesus, the miracle of resurrection—victory over physical and spiritual death—is now.

Like Lazarus, we all are dead in sin. We are stuck in a tomb—wrapped in our shortcomings and sins. It is impossible to break free on our own, but if we believe in Jesus, we are instantly freed from spiritual death and are alive in Jesus.

Jesus doesn't want to save you later. He wants to save you now! Jesus says to you what he said to Zacchaeus when they first met, "Today you... have been saved."[565] We don't have to wait to be saved. With Jesus, you are saved today.

Jesus's name is The Resurrection and The Life. Your new name is **immortal**. All who believe in Jesus are "raised to an immortal body . . . that they can die no more."[566] You are "alive unto God through Jesus Christ our Lord."[567] Resurrection is not a future event. It is a present reality.

Mitchell C. Taylor

Righteous Branch

Behold, the days come, saith the Lord, that I will raise unto David a righteous branch.
Jeremiah 23:5, King James Version

One night I was reading my scriptures in 2 Nephi 20. As I was reading, verse 15 really stood out to me. This verse is taken from Isaiah 10:15 which reads, "Is the axe to boast itself over the one who chops with it? Is the saw to exalt itself over the one who wields it? That would be like a club wielding those who lift it, Or like a rod lifting him who is not wood."[568] When I read this verse, the Lord gave me a vision.

In the vision, I was shown a saw that was being used by a man. As the man was using the saw, all of a sudden the tool revolted and started sawing off the man's arm. Once the saw had cut completely through the man's arm, the saw and the arm fell to the ground. The saw lay in the dirt until it became rusted and useless.

As I pondered the meaning of this vision, the following interpretation was given. We are all instruments in the hands of Lord and can't do anything without Him. John 15:5 teaches, "Without me ye can do nothing." Many, like the saw, want to be able to do things on their own and fight against the hand that makes them effective. As soon as they are severed from the source of their power, they become useless, rusty saws lying in the dirt.

When I saw that Jesus's name was Branch, I thought, aren't we the branches and Christ the roots? Jeremiah 23:5 answered my question. 'Branch' is translated from the word *tsemach*, which means sprout or bud. What Jeremiah was trying to teach is that Jesus is the source that will come. Jesus is the source of our power. He isn't the branches that protrude from the tree. He is the Branch that is the sprout—the beginning—the source.

Jesus is the Righteous Branch we extend from. He is the only source of life, joy, and salvation. If we aren't connected to the Righteous Branch, we will shrivel up and die. Without Him, we have no life. We become dead sticks lying on the ground.

Whom Say Ye that I Am?

Romans 11:17–18 reads, "[You] became a partaker of the root and fatness of the olive tree, 'But you must not brag . . . You are just a branch, not the root.'"[569] We need to remember that our source of nourishment and strength is Jesus—not ourselves. We are just branches. We are not the source. As we remember our dependence on God for survival, we will be nourished by Jesus and produce much fruit.

The Old Testament prophesied that a righteous branch would come forth from David. The branch was a symbol of the coming Messiah who was to save the Jews. Out of all the Sons of Jesse, God chose David, the youngest brother, to be the line the Messiah would come through. God uses the "foolish things of the world to confound the wise; and God hath chosen the weak things of the world to confound the things which are mighty."[570]

God uses weak things to clearly show who is the source and cause of the mighty miracles that are brought to pass. We don't perform miracles, but the Righteous Branch we are connected to does. Jesus is the source. Don't cut off the arm that is your source of power.

Jesus's name is Righteous Branch. Your new name is **alive**. Jesus "is the light and life of the world."[571] All who are connected to Him are "alive in Christ"[572] and "[partakers] of his goodness."[573]

Rock

The LORD is my rock, and my fortress, and my deliverer.
Psalm 18:2, King James Version

When we first moved to Idaho, my cousins and I loved to run up and down the dirt hills in our yards. One day, we decided to play a game where the people at the top of the hill rolled rocks down the hill, and the people at the bottom had to dodge them. I chose to be the person at the bottom who dodged all the rocks.

Everything was going well until one of my cousins decided to throw a large one at me. The rock landed directly on top of my head. I grabbed my head in stunned amazement. What had just happened? I took a moment to recover and thought I could continue playing until I looked at my hands. They were covered in blood! I went into panic mode and ran home as fast as I could, screaming for my mom.

While getting rocks chucked at your head isn't great—I still have a scar on the top of my head—building your life on a rock foundation is. When we build our lives on the solid foundation of Jesus, everything else falls into place.

Matthew chapter 16 records an interaction between Jesus and the apostle Peter. Jesus asked his disciples, "Whom say ye that I am?"[574] Peter answered, "Thou art the Christ, the Son of the living God."[575]

I can picture a big smile on Jesus's face as He replied, "You are blessed, Simon son of Jonah, because flesh and blood did not reveal this to you, but my Father in heaven! . . . And I say also unto thee, That thou art Peter, and upon this rock I will build my church; and the gates of hell shall not prevail against it."[576]

When Jesus said "upon this rock I will build my church," He wasn't referring to Peter as the rock or foundation. Peter or *Petros* means small stone. The word translated as rock in this scripture means bedrock. Jesus is telling Peter that the church will be built on the bedrock that Jesus is the Christ, the Son of the living God.

The bedrock of Jesus is the surest foundation we can build on. He is our source of strength in times of distress and danger. He is our refuge from the storm. Helaman 5:12 declares, "It is upon the rock of our Redeemer, who is Christ, the Son of God, that ye must build your foundation; that when the devil shall send forth his mighty winds, yea, his shafts in the whirlwind, yea, when all his hail and his mighty storm shall beat upon you, it shall have no power over you to drag you down to the gulf of misery and endless wo, because of the rock upon which ye are built, which is a sure foundation, a foundation whereon if men build they cannot fall."

This scripture doesn't say that we might not fall. It says we cannot fall. When we are founded upon Jesus, it is impossible to fall because Jesus will never fail. If Jesus is your foundation, no matter what the devil or anyone else throws at you, the scriptures promise that you will be immovable.

Jesus's name is Rock. Your new name is **steadfast**. Jesus "is the living God, and [is] steadfast forever."[577] Those who are with Him "cannot fall."[578]

Whom Say Ye that I Am?

Savior and Salvation

There shall be no other name given nor any other way nor means whereby salvation can come unto the children of men, only in and through the name of Christ, the Lord Omnipotent.
Mosiah 3:17

For my first book, *Perfect in Christ: The Good News of God's Grace*, I conducted a survey of active Latter-day Saints. One of the survey questions was "Do you want to go to the celestial kingdom?" And of course, one hundred percent of people answered, "Yes." I mean, who wouldn't want to go to the celestial kingdom? It's eternal life with Jesus. The next question on the survey was, "If you were to die today, at the Resurrection, would you go to the celestial kingdom?" The most common response to this question was, "I don't know." We want to go to the celestial kingdom, but we don't know if we are going. We don't know if we are saved. The answer to the question, "Am I saved and going to the celestial kingdom?" is found in Jesus.

One of Jesus's names is Savior. A savior is a person who saves, a deliverer, a helper. Jesus is our Savior from all things—sin, death, sickness, and anything else. He paid the price to save and rescue us. Acts 4:12 reads, "Neither is there salvation in any other: for there is none other name under heaven given among men, whereby we must be saved."[579] Only in the name of Jesus can we be saved.

We know Jesus is our Savior, but we don't know if we are saved and going to the celestial kingdom. A man in the New Testament named Zacchaeus had similar feelings. Zacchaeus wanted to be with Jesus, but he had a problem. He is a sinner. He was hated by the people because he was a tax collector and "had become very rich."[580] He was a traitor who stole from his people for the Romans and profited greatly from it.

When Zacchaeus heard that Jesus was going to pass by, he just wanted to see Him. But he knew Jesus would have a huge crowd around Him. He also knew it would be impossible for him to get close enough to see Jesus because he is hated by the people and extremely short. But Zacchaeus was determined to see Jesus. He climbed a sycamore tree in hopes of seeing Jesus as He passed by. He didn't care if Jesus saw him, but He didn't want to miss seeing the Savior.

While Zacchaeus was sitting in the tree, the unexpected happened. Jesus looked up and called out, "Zacchaeus, hurry down! I want to stay with you today."[581] "Zacchaeus quickly climbed down and took Jesus to his house in great excitement and joy."[582] After Jesus dined with Zacchaeus, He told him, "Today salvation has come to this house."[583]

Jesus had thousands of people walking alongside him. He could have chosen anyone from the crowd to eat with, but He chose a tax collector—an undeserving sinner.

When Jesus called to Zacchaeus, I bet there was a huge gasp. "What?! Jesus is going to Zacchaeus's house! He's a sinner who steals from us. He doesn't deserve this." Zacchaeus didn't deserve it, but that's what grace is—an undeserved gift.

Sometimes we all feel like Zacchaeus—cast out, unloved, and unwanted. But Jesus wants you. You might think, "I am unworthy. Jesus can't be with me." If you feel weak and unworthy, "Congratulations, you just made the lineup!"[584] We don't deserve Jesus coming to our house, but He comes. We simply have to let Him in and receive His gift of salvation. Salvation and exaltation are gifts to the unworthy and undeserving.

In Alma 26:36, Ammon calls Jesus, "My salvation." Salvation isn't an event, and it isn't something you earn. It's a relationship with our Savior, Jesus Christ. Salvation is a person. Jesus is the salvation that came to Zacchaeus's house.

Jesus doesn't save you later. He saves you now. Jesus said to Zacchaeus, "Today you . . . have been saved."[585] He didn't say tomorrow or sometime in the future. He said "today!" "The idea of being 'saved' to the ancient Hebrews was not a future salvation in the world to come, but an immediate salvation from any enemy, trouble or distress."[586] Jesus saves you today.

Jesus's name is Savior and Salvation. Your new name is **saved**. Acts 16:31 declares, "Believe on the Lord Jesus Christ, and you will be saved."[587] It doesn't say, "You might be saved," or "If you are really, really good, you will be saved." It says, "Believe on the Lord Jesus Christ, and you will be saved."[588] When you put your faith and trust in Jesus, you can say with confidence, "I am saved. I am going to the celestial kingdom."

Whom Say Ye that I Am?

Strength

*Trust you in the L*ORD *for ever: for in the*
*L*ORD J*EHOVAH is everlasting strength.*
Isaiah 26:4, American King James Version

In my family, we jokingly call my dad "small." In response, my dad looks us dead in the eyes and screams, "I'm not a small man!"

Like my dad, none of us want to be small or weak. We want to appear independent and strong, feeling big and important. But no matter how much we try or act like we have everything put together all the time, we somehow still feel weak. So we try harder, but that just makes us feel even worse. How can we stop feeling weak and find significance? Our answer is found in Jesus—whose name is Strength.

Have you ever wondered why life is hard or why Jesus let's bad things happen to you? One reason is to help you realize that you are weak and need help. We learn in Jacob 4:7, "The Lord God showeth us our weakness that we may know that it is by his grace, and his great condescensions unto the children of men, that we have power to do these things." The Lord allows hard things to happen to help draw us closer to Him—the only source of strength and success.

Jesus gives us weaknesses and trials to humble us and help us realize that we are weak. Jesus teaches, "I will show unto them their weakness. I give unto men weakness that they may be humble; and my grace is sufficient for all men that humble themselves before me; for if they humble themselves before me, and have faith in me, then will I make weak things become strong unto them."[589]

Jesus doesn't hate you or want you to suffer. It's actually the opposite. He allows hard things to happen so you will turn to Him and rely solely on Him. We need to be like Nephi and declare, "I have trusted in thee, and I will trust in thee forever. I will not put my trust in the arm of flesh; for I know that cursed is he that putteth his trust in the arm of flesh."[590] The arm of flesh is weak and will always fail us, but "[we] can do all things because Christ gives [us] the strength."[591]

The apostle Paul questioned why the Lord wouldn't relieve him of his burdens and trials. Jesus told Paul, "I am with you; that is all you need.

My power shows up best in weak people."[592] Paul then taught, "Now I am glad to boast about how weak I am; I am glad to be a living demonstration of Christ's power instead of showing off my own power and abilities. Since I know it is all for Christ's good, I am quite happy about 'the thorn,' and about insults and hardships, persecutions and difficulties; for when I am weak, then I am strong—the less I have, the more I depend on him."[593]

Jesus's name is Strength. Your new name is **strengthened**. When you "trust in the Lord,"[594] you will find "everlasting strength."[595] Be "confident and unafraid. For the Lord is [your] strength."[596]

Sure Foundation

Behold I lay in Zion . . . a sure foundation.
Isaiah 28:16, King James Version

As Jesus concluded the Sermon on the Mount, He taught this parable: "All who listen to my instructions and follow them are wise, like a man who builds his house on solid rock. Though the rain comes in torrents, and the floods rise and the storm winds beat against his house, it won't collapse, for it is built on rock. But those who hear my instructions and ignore them are foolish, like a man who builds his house on sand. For when the rains and floods come, and storm winds beat against his house, it will fall with a mighty crash."[597]

We can listen to and follow many people—Jesus, family, friends, parents, reporters, influencers, movie stars, YouTubers, teachers, authors, ministers, politicians, etc. What voices are you listening to and following?

According to a report published by researchers at the University of California San Diego, the average American consumes about one hundred thousand words per day, both those read in print and on the web as well as those heard from television, radio, and other interactions.[598] That's a lot of messages. Are you listening to the words of Jesus or the words of the world?

Whom Say Ye that I Am?

We are each building our foundation one word at a time. Listening to and following Jesus is how we build a sure foundation. Ignoring Jesus's instructions is foolish and like building on sand.

Initially the house built by the wise man and the house built by the foolish man looked similar, but when the rain and floods came, the houses were very different. The wise man's home stayed secure while the foolish man's home fell with a mighty crash. Jesus is "the only sure foundation."[599]

In our lives, the rains will come, the floods will rise, and trials and temptations will beat against us. To remain secure and stable, we need to be founded on the "rock of our redeemer"[600] by listening to and following Jesus.

The foundations of the world will eventually fail. When the storms and floods of life beat upon us, we discover the quality of our foundation. Those who have built a sandy foundation will be filled with fear and panic as their foundation crumples and their house collapses, but those who have built a Sure Foundation will have no need for fear or panic.

In Isaiah 28:16 we read, "He one who relies on [Jesus] will never be stricken with panic."[601] With Jesus as your foundation, you can have full confidence that it will remain firm and sure no matter the storm. Jesus is steadfast and immovable. Jesus will never fail. "The foundation of God standeth sure."[602]

The hymn "My Hope Is Built on Nothing Less" beautifully states, "My hope is built on nothing less than Jesus Christ, my righteousness; I dare not trust the sweetest frame, But wholly lean on Jesus' name. On Christ, the solid Rock, I stand; All other ground is sinking sand."

Jesus's name is Sure Foundation. Your new name is **solid**. "All who listen to [Jesus's] instructions and follow them are wise, like a man who builds his house on solid rock. Though the rain comes in torrents, and the floods rise and the storm winds beat against his house, it won't collapse, for it is built on rock."[603] You are firm, steadfast, and immovable.[604]

Mitchell C. Taylor

True Vine

I am the true vine[605]
—Jesus (John 15:1, King James Version)

Imagine that Jesus is about to share with you His final message. What would He say? How intensely would you listen?

The Bible records Jesus and His disciples' final meal together in an upper room on the evening before His crucifixion. For months Jesus tried to tell His apostles He was going to give His life, but the apostles didn't understand. They didn't think Jesus could be killed. They believed Jesus would always be with them, but Jesus knew that in less than twenty-four hours He would be crucified for the sins of the world. Following the meal now known as the last supper, Jesus declared that He would be betrayed and killed. The hope of Jesus always being with them was extinguished. The disciples were sad and confused. Jesus ended their time in the upper room by saying, "I am doing what the Father told Me to do . . . Come, let us be on our way."[606]

Eleven dejected men followed Jesus down the stairs and out into the cool night air. Some of the disciples carried lamps to light the way. Perhaps Jesus told them where He was headed—to a garden on the Mount of Olives where they often spent time. Perhaps they already knew. The disciples followed Jesus down the hill, through the winding streets of Jerusalem. Jesus led them out of the city to follow the Kidron Valley to their destination. Along the terraces that followed the curve of the valley, they passed through vineyards. They walked between rows of neatly tended grapes, plants that had been bearing fruit for generations. To their left the city walls of Jerusalem and to their right the Mount of Olives, where Gethsemane and betrayal awaited. Jesus stopped in the vineyard, and His disciples gathered around.[607]

What was Jesus's final message on the night before his death? It's often called the parable of the vine and is found in John chapter 15. As they were surrounded by vines, branches, and grapes, Jesus said, "I am the true vine, and my Father is the vinedresser. Every branch in me that does not bear fruit he takes away, and every branch that does bear fruit he prunes, that it may bear more fruit. Already you are clean because of the word that I have spoken to you. Abide in me, and I in you. As the branch cannot bear fruit by itself, unless it abides in the vine, neither can you, unless you abide in me. I am the vine; you are the branches. Whoever abides in me and I in him, he it is that bears much fruit, for apart from me you can do nothing . . . These things I have spoken to you . . . that your joy may be full."[608]

A vine is the base and source of nourishment. Jesus is the source. There is no source of life within us. It's only found in Jesus. Jesus declares, "I am the vine; you are the branches . . . without me ye can do nothing."[609] We can't accomplish anything independent of Jesus. We must be connected to Jesus, or we cannot survive. Without Jesus, we are just a dead withered branch.

Jesus says, "Whoever abides in me and I in him, he it is that bears much fruit."[610] If a branch wants to live and thrive, it must rely on the vine. Likewise, we must rely on Jesus. A branch that is connected to a tree is alive and bears fruit, not because it has power in itself, but because it's connected to the source.

What does it mean to abide with Jesus? Abiding is friendship. I think many followers of Christ are experts at serving God, but many have little experience being friends with God. Jesus wants to be our friend. Abiding with Jesus is a relationship, not a list of things to do.

Jesus wants each of us to be connected to Him. He invites us to enter a covenant relationship with Him through baptism. However, some believe every time we commit a sin, we are removed from the covenant and removed from our relationship with Jesus. If this were the case, Jesus's vine would just be a stump. There would be no branches because everyone sins. To be without sin is not the requirement to be with Jesus.

Some of these misunderstandings come from an inaccurate translation of John 15:2 which reads, "Every branch in me that does not bear fruit he takes away."[611] The Greek word which is translated to takes away is *airo*. A clearer translation . . . would be "take up" or "lift up." In both the Bible and Greek literature, *airo*, never means "cut off." It is unfortunate that some Bibles translate the word *airo* as "takes away" or "cut off."[612]

This explanation by an owner of a large vineyard in northern California brings understanding to grape branches being lifted. "New branches have a natural tendency to trail down and grow along the ground.

But they don't bear fruit down there. When branches grow along the ground, the leaves get coated in dust. When it rains, they get muddy and mildewed. The branch becomes sick and useless. [Do I] cut it off and throw it away? Oh, no! The branch is much too valuable for that. We go through the vineyard with a bucket of water looking for those branches. We lift them up and wash them off. Then we wrap them around the trellis or tie them up. Pretty soon they're thriving."[613]

"When the branches fall into the dirt, God doesn't throw them away or abandon them. He lifts them up, cleans them off, and helps them flourish again."[614]

I can picture Jesus taking the branches in the dirt and lifting and cleaning them as he taught His disciples. The verse following His explanation of lifting the branches, Jesus declares the good news, "You are clean."[615]

Jesus doesn't take us away or cut us off. He lifts us. He cleans us. We don't have to be discouraged by thinking that, when we sin, Jesus cuts us off and we are no longer on His team. Making mistakes is a part of life. I am grateful Jesus is merciful and lets me stay with Him. Jesus is our source of life, and because of Him, we are alive and clean.

Jesus's name is True Vine. Your new name is **lively**. Jesus has saved you, and "according to his abundant mercy hath begotten [you] again unto a lively hope by the resurrection of Jesus Christ from the dead."[616] When you are with Jesus, "you are clean"[617] and "your cup of joy will overflow!"[618]

Witness

To this end was I born, and for this cause came I into the world, that I should bear witness unto the truth.[619]
—Jesus (John 18:37, King James Version)

Have you ever wondered what it would be like to be a witness in court and tell what you know to help the judge or jury reach a verdict? I think it would be awesome, but also super nerve-racking. I would be afraid of jumbling my words and coming off as if I were lying.

Whom Say Ye that I Am?

While Jesus doesn't ask us to be a witness in court, He does ask us to be a witness of Him! Once we join Jesus's family, we help bring others to Jesus. Jesus wants us to "go into all the world and preach the good news to everyone."[620] The apostle Paul declares, "We are witnesses of all things which [Jesus] did both in the land of the Jews, and in Jerusalem; whom they slew and hanged on a tree . . . that through his name whosoever believeth in him shall receive remission of sins."[621]

We are to tell everyone that Jesus lives and has forgiven them of all their sins. We are to tell everyone that Jesus loves them and gave His life to save them. What better message is there than that? Jesus gives you this promise, "You will receive power . . . and you will be my witnesses, telling people about me everywhere."[622] We are to tell people about all that Jesus has done for us and "everything that has happened."[623]

Sharing our witness of Jesus brings others to Jesus, and Jesus promises to be our witness to Heavenly Father that we belong to Him and are thus innocent. Jesus declares, "If anyone publicly acknowledges me as his friend . . . I will say before my Father in heaven that they belong to me . . . [and are] innocent before God."[624]

The Bible tells us that "Jesus . . . is the faithful witness."[625] Jesus is a witness who only speaks the truth. You can believe Him. You can trust Him. Jesus is the one and only "faithful and true witness."[626] Regardless of how much time passes or what circumstances we are in, Jesus is "the same yesterday, to day, and for ever."[627]

When we obey the command to "preach [the] gospel unto every creature who has not received it,"[628] we bear witness of the Witness, and the Witness bears perfect testimony of our innocence to the Father.

Jesus's name is Witness. Your new name is **innocent**. Whenever questions or doubts come about your worthiness, remember this testimony of Jesus: "Your sins are forgiven you; you are clean before me; therefore, lift up your heads and rejoice."[629] You can believe with full trust and confidence that Jesus will declare your innocence to God.

Mitchell C. Taylor

Wonderful

His name shall be called Wonderful.
Isaiah 9:6, King James Version

In Isaiah 9:6, Isaiah prophesied of the birth of the Messiah and revealed that one of His names is Wonderful. Every time I read this verse, the word "wonderful" catches my attention. I totally agree that Jesus is Wonderful, but why? Of all the names Isaiah could have used, why did he choose Wonderful?

'Wonderful' is translated from the Hebrew word *pele,* which means a marvelous thing, a wonder. Jesus is a marvelous gift from God. Without Jesus, we are lost and fallen with nowhere to go. We don't deserve Jesus, but Heavenly Father loves us so much He sent His Son to save us. "For God so loved the world that he gave his only begotten son, that whosoever believeth in him should not perish but have everlasting life."[630] We are saved and redeemed because of the wonderful gift of Jesus. We are the luckiest people alive. No wonder Isaiah calls Jesus Wonderful.

Another meaning of the Hebrew word *pele* is a miracle. Jesus's birth to the virgin Mary was a miracle. His life, death, and resurrection were miracles. Jesus is a wonderful miracle, who performs great and mighty miracles in our lives. Jesus is a God of miracles.

The Hebrew word *pele* is derived from the Hebrew word *pala,* which means separate from all else. Heavenly Father and Jesus are incomparable Gods. There is nothing like them. Nothing can compare to Heavenly Father and our Wonderful friend, Jesus.

You are loved, cherished, and invaluable to Heavenly Father and Jesus. "The worth of souls is great in the sight of God; For, behold, the Lord your Redeemer suffered death in the flesh; wherefore he suffered the pain of all men, that all men might . . . come unto him . . . and be saved."[631]

Jesus's name is Wonderful. Your new name is **priceless**. You are saved and redeemed because of the wonderful gift of Jesus. Rejoice in "the Lord, and his strength, and his wonderful works."[632] "Praise the LORD for his goodness, and for his wonderful works."[633]

Whom Say Ye that I Am?

Word

*In the beginning was the Word, and the Word
was with God, and the Word was God.*
John 1:1, King James Version

I love the vision of the tree of life. After Lehi told his family about the vision, Laman and Lemuel were very confused and blasted a bunch of questions at Nephi. One of the questions they asked was "What meaneth the rod of iron?"[634] Nephi answered them saying, "[The iron rod is] the word of God."[635]

When people first read that the iron rod is the word of God, they often assume Nephi is talking about the scriptures. However, this is not the case. Many scriptures refer to Jesus as the Word, including 1 John 5:7 which reads, "For there are three that bear record in heaven, the Father, the Word, and the Holy Ghost: and these three are one."[636]

In 1 Nephi 15:24, Nephi says, ". . . give heed to the word of God and remember to keep his commandments always in all things." If Nephi was talking about the scriptures when he said "the word of God," why did he say *his* commandments instead of *its* commands? Because the word of God is a person not an object. We don't put our trust in a manuscript. We put our trust in a person named Jesus who is the Word of God. The iron rod that we cling to and are led by is Jesus.

In the New Testament, the word "Word" is translated from the Greek word *logos,* meaning divine expression or speaker. In New Testament times, the word *logos* was used to define the force behind the universe.[637] When the apostle John referred to Jesus as the Word, he was saying that Jesus is the divine force of the universe who is over and in all things.

In Jewish culture it was taught that God's word made things happen. Whatever words God spoke came to pass. Referring to Jesus as the Word was to call Him the God who speaks and makes things happen. It's through His spoken word that all things come to pass.

During the vision of the tree of life, Nephi saw the mortal ministry of Jesus. He described what he saw saying, "I beheld the Lamb of God going forth among the children of men. And I beheld multitudes of people who were sick, and who were afflicted with all manner of diseases, and with devils and unclean spirits; and the angel spake and showed all these things unto me. And they were healed by the power of the Lamb of God; and the devils and the unclean spirits were cast out . . . [and] he was lifted up upon the cross and slain for the sins of the world."[638]

Did Nephi see the scriptures performing miracles? No. He saw Jesus—the Word of God performing miracles!

Do the scriptures heal the sick? No, Jesus does.

Do the scriptures cast out devils? No, Jesus does.

Do the scriptures forgive your sins? No, Jesus does.

Did the scriptures hang on the cross? No, Jesus did.

We don't look to the scriptures for forgiveness or healing. We look to Jesus who "is clothed in a robe dipped in blood, and the name by which he is called is The Word of God."[639]

The iron rod who heals us, forgives us, and leads us to eternal life is Jesus. When we hold onto the iron rod, we aren't holding on to the scriptures. We are holding onto Jesus.

Jesus's name is Word. Your new name is **led**. When you lay "hold upon the word of God [Jesus]," you are able to "divide asunder all . . . the snares . . . of the devil, and [you are led] in a strait and narrow course across that everlasting gulf of misery [and your] immortal soul [lands] at the right hand of God in the kingdom of heaven, to sit down with Abraham, and Isaac, and with Jacob, and with all our holy fathers."[640]

Conclusion: Remember Who You Are

Remember the worth of souls is great in the sight of God.
Doctrine and Covenants 18:10

One of my all-time favorite movies is *The Lion King*—the original, not the live action. After Mufasa died, Simba was told by Scar to run away and never return. Simba ran and ran until he was far away from home where Scar began his reign as king. As Simba grew older, he forgot he was the rightful heir to the throne. As Simba went through a little midlife crisis, he heard in the clouds his father's deep voice echo through the savanna saying, "Simba, remember who you are." Simba remembered who he was. He returned home, dethroned Scar, and took his rightful spot as king.

Like Simba, we sometimes forget who we truly are. Scar tricks Simba into running away from home. Similarly, Satan tries to lead us away from our true identity, which is found in Jesus. Satan bombards us with doubt, confusion, and anxiety to prevent us from learning our divine heritage. When we don't know our identity in Jesus, Satan can deceive us into believing we are worthless, not good enough, and unloved. Satan knows that if you find your identity in Jesus, he won't be able to manipulate you. 1 Peter 5:8 declares, "Stay alert! Watch out for your great enemy, the devil. He prowls around like a roaring lion, looking for someone to devour."[641]

Satan "seeketh that all men [and women] might be miserable like unto himself."[642] You need to remember your true identity in Jesus. Jesus doesn't call us by our sins or shortcomings. He calls you by name. When Jesus returns, he will be asked, "What are these wounds in thine hands?

Then he shall answer, Those with which I was wounded in the house of my friends."[643]

Jesus didn't call those who turned Him in to be tortured and killed sinners, subjects, evil people, or ex-friends. He called them friends. Whenever Satan declares, "You are unloved," remember this scripture. Jesus loves you and is your friend no matter what.

Jesus didn't call Peter a doubter. He called him by name and eats with him.[644]

Jesus didn't call Saul a murderer. He called him by name and proclaims that he is a chosen vessel.[645]

Jesus didn't call Alma a persecutor. He called him by name and forgives his sins.[646]

Jesus didn't call Joseph Smith uneducated. He called him by name and restored His church through him.[647]

Jesus will never define you or call you by your past sins. He will call you by name and remind you of who you truly are. Peter isn't a doubter. He's a faithful witness. Saul isn't a murderer. He's a champion of grace. Alma isn't a persecutor. He's a mighty missionary. Joseph Smith isn't uneducated. He's the Lord's prophet. In Jesus, our past no longer defines us. We are perfect in Christ and called by His names. No matter your past, with Jesus, you have a beautiful future.

Identity is Crucial

During the COVID-19 pandemic, everyone had to wear masks. Masks hide one of the most crucial parts of humanity—our identity. Everyone's unique face and beautiful smile were hidden, making people hard to identify. At times I didn't recognize some of my closest friends because they were wearing masks that hid their identity.

Satan has devised a strategy to hide our identity in Jesus. He covers us with false labels such as "not worthy," "not good enough," "alone," "unwanted," and "unloved." To counteract Satan's false labels, I have created a list of all the names of Jesus. Next to Jesus's names, I have placed our new names to remind us of our identity in Christ. When you begin to feel discouraged, depressed, or anxious, look to see what Jesus calls you.

Satan says, "You are worthless," but Immanuel says, "You are precious in My sight."[648]

Whom Say Ye that I Am?

Satan says, "You aren't good enough," but the Great High Priest says, "You are worthy."

Satan bombards us with doubt, depression, and fear, but our Hope, Counselor, and Confidence assures us that everything will be alright. Look to Jesus for your identity, and you will see who you truly are!

Feeling?	Jesus Is	You Are	SCRIPTURE
Condemned	Your Advocate	Triumphant	D&C 43:3–5
Weak	Almighty	Strong	Psalm 28:7
Insignificant	Alpha and Omega	Eternal	Matthew 28:20
Ignored	The Amen	Answered	Mark 11:24
Useless	The Apostle	a Witness	D&C 33:8
Forgotten	The Author and Finisher	Wanted	Moses 1:39
Unloved	The Beloved	Loved	John 3:16
Empty	Your Bread of Life	Filled	John 6:49, 51
Not Good Enough	Your Bridegroom	Good Enough	Colossians 1:28
Astray	The Bright and Morning Star	Guided	Psalm 119:105
Misled	Your Captain of Salvation	Directed	2 Nephi 32:3
Broken	Your Carpenter	Whole	Isaiah 53:5
Unstable	The Chief Cornerstone	Immovable	Helaman 5:12
Useless	The Christ & Your Messiah	Set Apart	Romans 8:16
Defeated	Your Commander	Victorious	1 Corinthians 15:57
Fear	Your Confidence	Confident	Isaiah 41:10
Depressed	Your Counselor	Comforted	Alma 37:36–37
Unwanted	Your Creator	a Child of God	Deuteronomy 4:31
Enslaved	Your Deliverer	Delivered	Joel 2:32
Insufficient	The Door	Abundant	John 10:10
Starved	El Shaddai	Nourished	2 Nephi 2:25
Sad	El Simkhat Gili	Delighted	Matthew 6:33
Abandoned	The Everlasting Father	Family (Haniai)	John 14:18

Whom Say Ye that I Am?

Feeling?	Jesus Is	You Are	SCRIPTURE
Deserted	Your Exemplar	Exemplary	1 Peter 2:21
Defenseless	The Firstborn	Defended	John 15:13
Friendless	a Friend of Sinners	His Friend	John 15:14
Unfavored	The Gift	Blessed	Romans 6:23
Unknown	God	Known	JSH 1:17
Lost	The Good Shepherd	Found	Luke 19:10
Powerless	The Governor	Powerful	Matthew 17:20
Condemned	Grace	Justified	Romans 3:24
Inadequate	The Great High Priest	Worthy	Luke 21:36
Defeated	Greater	an Overcomer	1 John 4:4
Accused	Holy, Holy, Holy	Blameless	1 Thessalonians 3:1
Hopeless	Hope	Hopeful	2 Nephi 4:19
Unforgiven	The Great I AM	Forgiven	D&C 50:36
Worthless	Immanuel	Precious	D&C 18:10
Trapped	Jesus	Rescued	Jeremiah 15:21
Doubt	Jesus of Nazareth	Assured	Psalm 111:3
Guilty	The Judge	Not Guilty	Romans 8:1
Excluded	The Keeper of the Gate	Admitted	2 Nephi 26:33
Less Than	King	an Heir	Titus 3:7
Unclean	The Lamb of God	Clean	1 Nephi 12:10
Ineligible	The Lawgiver	His Disciple	2 Corinthians 3:18
Darkness	The Light of the World	a Conqueror	D&C 10:5
Judged	The Lion of Judah	Understood	Alma 7:12
Worried	LORD	Secure	John 10:28
Sacred	The Lord of Hosts	Protected	D&C 84:88
Prideful	Lord of the Sabbath	Humble	Matthew 5:3

Feeling?	Jesus Is	You Are	SCRIPTURE
Sorrow	Man of Sorrows	Joyful	D&C 110:5
Disorder	Your Master	Servant	D&C 4:2
Pain	Your Mediator	Relieved	Galatians 3:13
Shut Out	Meek and Lowly	Exalted	Matthew 5:3
Helpless	The Mighty God	Unbeatable	Zephaniah 3:17
Confined	Omnipotent	Unlimited	Philippians 4:13
Divided	One	Unified	John 17:21–22
Punished	Your Passover	Spared	Romans 4:7
Unworthy	Perfection	Perfect	Romans 8:1
Sick	Your Physician	Healed	Psalm 147:3
Stagnate	The Potter	Transformed	Philippians 3:21
Distress	The Prince of Peace	Peaceful	John 14:27
Out of Place	The Prophet	Watched Over	D&C 101:54
Doubtful	Your Rabbi	a Believer	Mosiah 4:9
Fallen	Your Redeemer	Redeemed	Titus 2:14
Anxiety	Rest	Serene	Matthew 11:28–30
Finite	The Resurrection & The Life	Immortal	Alma 11:45
Dead	The Righteous Branch	Alive	2 Nephi 25:25
Shaky	Your Rock	Steadfast	1 Peter 5:10
Unsure	Your Savior	Saved	Acts 16:31
Small	Strength	Strengthened	2 Nephi 2:22
Unsteady	Your Sure Foundation	Solid	Nahum 1:7
Disconnected	The True Vine	Lively	1 Peter 1:3
Shame	Your Witness	Innocent	D&C 93:38
Meaningless	Wonderful	Priceless	D&C 18:10–11
Confused	The Word	Led	Enos 1:15

Whom Say Ye that I Am?

These are written, that ye might believe that Jesus is the Christ, the Son of God; and that believing ye might have life through his name.

John 20:31, King James Version

Those who know your name trust in you.

Psalm 9:10, New International Version

Endnotes

Amplified Bible (AB)
Aramaic Bible in Plain English (ABPE)
Berean Literal Bible (BLB)
Berean Study Bible (BSB)
Christian Standard Bible (CSB)
Contemporary English Version (CEV)
Darby Bible Translation (DBT)
Disciples' Literal New Testament (DLNT)
Easy-to-Read Version (EtRV)
English Revised Version (ERV)
English Standard Version (ESV)
English Standard Version Anglicised (ESVA)
GOD'S WORD Translation (GWT)
Good News Translation (GNT)
Holman Christian Standard Bible (HCSB)
International Standard Version (ISV)
Jubilee Bible (JUB)
King James Version (KJV)
Modern English Version (MEV)
New American Standard Bible (NASB)
New Century Version (NCV)
New English Translation (NET)
New Heart English Bible (NHEB)
New International Version (NIV)
New International Reader's Version (NIRV)
New King James Version (NKJV)
New Life Version (NLV)
New Living Translation (NLT)
Peshitta Holy Bible Translated (PHBT)
The Living Bible (TLB)
The Message (TM)
The Passion Translation (PT)
Tree of Life Version (TLV)
Webster's Bible Translation (WBT)
Word English Bible (WEB)

1 Exodus 20:13, JUB 2000.
2 Spiros Zodhiates, Th.D, *The Complete Word Study New Testament*, AMG International, Inc., 1991), 882.
3 Luke 18:13, KJV.
4 Matthew 14:30, KJV.
5 Dieter F. Uchtdorf, "The Gift of Grace," *General Conference*, April 2015.
6 Stephen Robinson, *Believing Christ: Reflections*, Lectures on Grace, BYU Wheatley Institution, Dec. 1, 2017.
7 Mark 8:27, KJV.
8 Mark 8:28, KJV.
9 Matthew 16:15, KJV.
10 Jeremiah 29:13, NASB.
11 Isaiah 43:1, NASB.
12 C.S. Lewis, *Mere Christianity* (United Kingdom: HarperCollins, 2001), 52.
13 Gospel Library App, The Bible, Matthew 25:12, Footnote A, Joseph Smith Translation & Inspired Version Mathew 25:11.
14 John 14:5, KJV.
15 1 Corinthians 12:3, NET.
16 Matthew 16:17, TLB.
17 Moroni 10:5.
18 Matthew 16:17, KJV.
19 John 6:69, ABPE.
20 Ether 12:27.
21 Isaiah 56:5, NLT.
22 Revelation 3:12, KJV.
23 Alma 5:38.
24 John 8:32, ISV.
25 Acts 4:12, ESV.
26 John 17:3, NLT.
27 Jeffrey R. Holland, *Witness for His Names* (Salt Lake City, UT: Deseret

Book, 2019), 12.
28 Robert J. Morgan, *He Shall Be Called* (Warner Faith, 2005), xiii.
29 Matthew 16:15, KJV.
30 Max Lucado, *In the Manger* (Nashville, TN: Thomas Nelson, 2012), 84–86.
31 Philippians 2:10-11, NASB.
32 Romans 3:23, NIV.
33 Alma 9:11.
34 Romans 8:1, NIV.
35 Colossians 2:14, CEV.
36 John 3:17-18, KJV.
37 John 8:10–11, KJV.
38 Doctrine and Covenants 45:3–5.
39 Doctrine and Covenants 76:39.
40 2 Corinthians 2:14, KJV.
41 Job 9:10, NIV.
42 Moses1:1–3.
43 Moses 1:10.
44 Mosiah 2:25.
45 John 15:5, KJV.
46 Matthew 17:20.
47 Jeremiah 32:17, NIV.
48 Psalm 28:7, ESV.
49 Philippians 4:13, NKJV.
50 Luke 1:37, NHEB.
51 Ryan K. Olson. *The Answer is Jesus*. General Conference, Salt Lake City: The Church of Jesus Christ of Latter-day Saints, October 2022.
52 Doctrine and Covenants 88:106.
53 Moses 2:1.
54 Genesis 1:26–27, KJV.
55 John 5:30.
56 Matthew 28:20, KJV.
57 Mark 14:36, ESV.
58 2 Corinthians 1:20, KJV.
59 Enos 1:6.
60 Mark 11:24, GNT.
61 Matthew 21:22, NASB 1995; Matthew 7:7, NIV.
62 John 20:21, ASV.
63 Romans 14:11, NLT.
64 1 Nephi 3:7.
65 Doctrine and Covenants 88:106.
66 Moses 1:39.
67 Matthew 3:17; Matthew 17:5; 2 Peter 1:17; JSH 1:17.
68 John 3:16, KJV.
69 John 6:35, KJV.
70 Exodus 25:23–30; Leviticus 24:5–9.
71 John 6:9, KJV.
72 John 6:51, KJV.
73 John 6:35, KJV; John 6:29, NLT; John 6:47, KJV.
74 John 6:41–42, King James Version.
75 John 6:66.
76 John 6:35, CSB.
77 John 6:49.
78 John 6:48, KJV.
79 Romans 15:13, NLT.
80 John 6:35, NIV.
81 Matthew 25:11, KJV.
82 Matthew 25:11, Inspired Version, Joseph Smith Translation.
83 Stephen E. Robinson. *Believing Christ* (Salt Lake City, UT: Deseret Book, 1992), 24–25.
84 2 Nephi 9:14.
85 Helaman 14:5.
86 Psalm 119:105, ESV.
87 John 8:12, BSB.
88 John 9:5, KJV.
89 John 14:6, KJV.
90 Alma 7:14.
91 Mark 4:38, ERV.
92 Mark 4:39, ESV.

93 Mark 4:39, ESV.
94 Mark 4:41, KJV.
95 Mark 4:40, KJV.
96 2 Nephi 32:3.
97 Mark 6:2, BSB.
98 Mark 6:3, KJV.
99 Revelation 3:17, NIV.
100 "Architectural Cornerstones: The Meaning, History, and Intent," *NewStudio Architecture*, June 3, 2019, Retrieved October 28, 2021 from https://www.newstudioarchitecture.com/newstudio-insights/architectural-cornerstones.
101 Helaman 5:12.
102 1 Peter 2:8, KJV.
103 Helaman 5:12.
104 1 Peter 2:6, WEB.
105 Luke 1:31, NLT.
106 1 Peter 1:20.
107 Matthew 16:13, KJV.
108 Matthew 16:14, KJV.
109 Matthew 16:15, KJV.
110 Matthew 16:16, KJV.
111 Jarom 1:11.
112 Isaiah 43:1.
113 John 18:36.
114 Doctrine and Covenants 78:18.
115 Matthew 8:7, KJV.
116 Matthew 8:8–9, KJV.
117 Matthew 8:13, KJV.
118 Moses 1:10.
119 John 2:5, BLB.
120 Zephaniah 3:17, GWT.
121 Doctrine and Covenants 104:82.
122 2 Nephi 4:19.
123 2 Timothy 4:7, NLT.
124 John 19:30, NLT.
125 1 Corinthians 15:54, GNT.
126 Philippians 3:3, NLT.
127 Psalm 65:5, ISV.
128 Toni Sorenson, *12 Steps Closer to Christ: Activating the Atonement for Spiritual Healing* (American Fork, UT: Covenant Communications Incorporated, 2015).
129 1 John 2:28, BSB.
130 Hebrews 10:35, ESVA.
131 Psalm 27:3, TLB.
132 John 14:18, KJV.
133 John 1:3, KJV.
134 Mosiah 3:8.
135 Genesis 1:26.
136 Moses 1:39
137 John H. Groberg, *The Fire of Faith* (Salt Lake City: Deseret Book, 1996) 302.
138 John 15:5, KJV.
139 2 Nephi 2:25.
140 Psalm 81:7, ESV.
141 Matthew 18:11, ISV.
142 Joel 2:32, NET.
143 John 10:7, KJV.
144 1 Nephi 8:21.
145 1 Nephi 8:23.
146 1 Nephi 8:30.
147 John 10:7, KJV; John 10:1 KJV.
148 Acts 4:12, BSB.
149 Psalm 3:8, ESV.
150 John 10:5, NET.
151 Mosiah 3:17.
152 John 10:10, KJV.
153 Jeff A. Benner, *His Name Is One* (self-published, 2002), 43.
154 Jeff A. Benner, *His Name Is One* (self-published, 2002), 43.
155 John 10:10, PT.
156 Genesis 50:21; Matthew 6:33, NLT.
157 Matthew 27:46, NLT.

Whom Say Ye that I Am?

158 Psalm 43:1–5, NLT.
159 Psalm 43:1–5, NLT.
160 Russell M. Nelson, "Joy and Spiritual Survival," *General Conference,* October 2016.
161 Psalm 43:1–5, NLT.
162 3 Nephi 1:13; Matthew 9:2; Matthew 14:27; John 16:33.
163 Romans 15:13, PT.
164 Jeremiah 31:13, NIV.
165 Proverbs 29:17, NHEB.
166 Psalm 35:9, KJV.
167 Isaiah 43:1, NASB.
168 Hebrews 13:5, ISV.
169 John 12:32, GNT.
170 Doctrine and Covenants 84:38.
171 John 14:18, NLT.
172 Acts 10:38.
173 Romans 5:8, NLT.
174 2 Nephi 31:16.
175 Doctrine and Covenants 6:36.
176 Proverbs 3:5, ISV.
177 2 Nephi 32:3.
178 Russell M. Nelson, "Revelation for the Church, Revelation for Our Lives," *General Conference,* April 2018.
179 Matthew 5:16, ESV.
180 Doctrine and Covenants 93:21.
181 John 15:13, NASB.
182 Helaman 5:12.
183 Deuteronomy 32:4, GNT.
184 Matthew 18:11, HCSB.
185 Matthew 11:28, ABPE.
186 Romans 3:10, GNT.
187 Matthew 9:13, NLT.
188 Alma 38:14.
189 1 John 1:8, KJV.
190 Romans 3:10, KJV.
191 Matthew 26:6–13, KJV.
192 Matthew 26:13, KJV.
193 John 15:14, CSB.
194 Revelation 3:20, NLT.
195 John 3:16, KJV.
196 Matthew 20:28, NIV.
197 1 Timothy 4:14, NIV.
198 Romans 6:23, ISV.
199 2 Corinthians 9:15, NASB.
200 "The One True God" Retrieved May 4, 2022 from https://doctrine.org/the-one-true-god.
201 Isaiah 44:8, NIV.
202 Exodus 20:3, KJV.
203 Joseph Smith History 1:17.
204 Exodus 33:17, ESV.
205 Genesis 35:11; Genesis 46:3; Psalm 46:10; Psalm 50:7; Isaiah 43:12; Isaiah 45:22; Isaiah 46:9; Hosea 11:9; Revelation 1:8, CEV; 2 Nephi 27:23; 2 Nephi 29:8; 2 Nephi 29:14; Helaman 10:6; Doctrine and Covenants 1:24; Doctrine and Covenants 6:2; Doctrine and Covenants 11:2; Doctrine and Covenants 12:2; Doctrine and Covenants 14:2; Doctrine and Covenants 35:8; Doctrine and Covenants 49:5; Doctrine and Covenants 63:6; Doctrine and Covenants 101:16; Moses 2:2; Moses 6:51; Moses 7:35.
206 Jeff A. Benner, *His Name Is One* (self-published, 2002), 97.
207 John 10:12, BSB.
208 Ezekiel 34:2, NLT.
209 John 10:4, NIV.
210 John 6:68, KJV.
211 John 17:3, NLT.
212 John R. Lasater, "Shepherds of Israel," *Ensign, May 1988.*
213 John 10:28, GWT.

214 Genesis 42:6, KJV.
215 C.S. Lewis, *Mere Christianity* (London: Harper Collins Publishers Ltd., 1996), 191.
216 C.S. Lewis, *Mere Christianity* (London: Harper Collins Publishers Ltd., 1996), 190–91.
217 2 Nephi 2:25.
218 Matthew 17:20, NIV.
219 Galatians 2:20, ERV; Galatians 2:21, WBT.
220 2 Corinthians 12:9, Ether 12:26, Moroni 10:32.
221 Ephesians 2:8, KJV.
222 2 Nephi 25:23.
223 Rich Wilkerson, Jr., *Friend of Sinners* (Nashville, TN: Thomas Nelson, 2018), 14.
224 Romans 3:24, NIV.
225 Doctrine and Covenants 110:5.
226 Alma 34:8–15.
227 Matthew 5:17, GNT.
228 Matthew 3:15, KJV.
229 Mark 15:38, NASB.
230 Hebrews 4:16, NET.
231 Hebrews 9:12, NLT.
232 2 Nephi 9:14.
233 Luke 21:36, KJV.
234 Matthew 25:21, NKJV.
235 Doctrine and Covenants 78:18.
236 Luke 18:10–14, TLB.
237 Luke 18:9, TM.
238 Mosiah 4:2.
239 Alma 38:14.
240 John 15:5, CSB.
241 1 John 5:5, NIV.
242 1 John 5:4, AB.
243 Doctrine and Covenants 88:106.
244 John 16:33, AB.
245 Job 33:12, KJV.
246 John 13:16, John 6:26, John 14:12, KJV.
247 Revelations 4:8, BLB.
248 1 Peter 1:16, NLT.
249 Romans 3:23.
250 Alma 45:16.
251 1 Thessalonians 3:13, NIV.
252 Ephesians 4:14, NIV.
253 2 Nephi 31:20.
254 Psalm 33:17, ESV.
255 1 Peter 1:3, KJV.
256 Titus 1:2, KJV.
257 Romans 15:13, GWT.
258 Alma 46:15; Romans 8:24, WBT.
259 2 Nephi 4:19.
260 Exodus 3:10, BSB.
261 Exodus 3:13, ESV.
262 Exodus 3:14, CSB.
263 G.H. Parke-Taylor, *Yahweh: The Divine Name in the Bible* (Waterloo, Ontario: Wilfrid Laurier University Press, 1975), 51–52.
264 Doctrine and Covenants 38:2.
265 2 Nephi 2:25.
266 Matthew 6:34, KJV.
267 Matthew 6:34, TLB.
268 John 21:25, GWT.
269 Romans 10:9, NLT.
270 Luke 5:20, NIV.
271 Matthew 9:5, ESV.
272 Romans 10:13, NLT.
273 Doctrine and Covenants 50:36.
274 Psalm 107:4, NLT.
275 Isaiah 49:16, ESV.
276 Deuteronomy 31:8, ESV.
277 Matthew 28:20, NLT.
278 Tony Evans, *Power of Jesus' Names* (Eugene, OR: Harvest House Publishers, 2019), 24.

Whom Say Ye that I Am?

279 Isaiah 43:4, NLT.
280 Acts 4:12, NLT.
281 Isaiah 41:10, ISV.
282 Jeff A. Benner, *His Name Is One* (self-published, 2002), 4.
283 Matthew 18:11.
284 Jeremiah 15:21 NIV; Jeremiah 15:21, NLT.
285 Matthew 2:23, KJV.
286 John 1:46.
287 John 18:4, KJV.
288 John 18:5, KJV.
289 John 18:5, KJV.
290 John 18:6, KJV.
291 Luke 22:51.
292 Luke 23:21, BSB.
293 Isaiah 61:3.
294 1 Timothy 3:13, NIV.
295 Psalm 111:3, NLT.
296 Alma 28:11.
297 Romans 3:10, GNT.
298 Jeff A. Benner, *His Name Is One* (self-published, 2002), 61–62.
299 Elder J. Devn Cornish, "Am I Good Enough? Will I Make It?" *General Conference*, April 2016.
300 Elder J. Devn Cornish, "Am I Good Enough? Will I Make It?" *General Conference*, April 2016.
301 Alma 42:13.
302 Mosiah 15:9; Alma 34:14–16.
303 1 John 4:19, KJV.
304 Romans 3:23, KJV.
305 Romans 5:20, CEV.
306 Isaiah 53:5, TLB; Romans 8:1, HCSB.
307 2 Nephi 26:33.
308 Matthew 7:23, Joseph Smith Translation.
309 Matthew 11:28, NIV.
310 2 Nephi 26:33.
311 Mosiah 5:8.
312 Mosiah 4:6.
313 Jeff A. Benner, *His Name Is One* (self-published, 2002), 76-77.
314 Jeff A. Benner, *His Name Is One* (self-published, 2002), 77.
315 3 Nephi 9:20.
316 Psalm 34:18, KJV.
317 2 Nephi 2:6–7.
318 Doctrine and Covenants 21:9.
319 Matthew 23:11, CEV.
320 Titus 2:14, NLT.
321 Moses 1:33.
322 Romans 8:17.
323 4 Nephi 1:17.
324 James 2:5, ESV.
325 Titus 3:7, PT.
326 John 1:29, KJV.
327 Genesis 15:2, CEV.
328 Genesis 21:2–3.
329 Genesis 22, CEV.
330 Genesis 22:3, KJV.
331 Genesis 22:7, KJV.
332 Genesis 22:8, KJV.
333 Genesis 22:12, NLT.
334 Genesis 22:13, CSB.
335 Doctrine and Covenants 19:16–17.
336 Hebrews 10:18, PT; Hebrews 10:18, NLT.
337 Matthew 20:28, CEV.
338 Doctrine and Covenants 88:106.
339 2 Nephi 2:23.
340 Moses 4:27.
341 2 Nephi 9:14.
342 2 Nephi 9:14.
343 1 Nephi 12:10.
344 The Declaration of Independence.
345 Doctrine and Covenants 38:22.

346 Doctrine and Covenants 122:7.
347 2 Nephi 2:24.
348 John 14:15, GNT.
349 3 Nephi 15:9.
350 Doctrine and Covenants 50:24.
351 2 Corinthians 3:18, TLB.
352 John 8:31–32, NET.
353 John 8:12, KJV.
354 John 8:12, GNT.
355 Psalm 119:105, NIV.
356 Daniel 2:22, TLB.
357 Acts 3:16, NIV; Doctrine and Covenants 10:5.
358 Revelations 5:2, NIV.
359 Revelations 5:3, NLT.
360 Revelations 5:4, ESV.
361 Revelations 5:5, NLT.
362 Revelations 5:6, ESV.
363 Doctrine and Covenants 122:8.
364 Revelations 5:12, NET.
365 Revelations 5:5, NLT.
366 3 Nephi 11:11; Alma 7:12.
367 Isaiah 42:8, KJV.
368 John 1:3.
369 Tony Evans, *Power of Jesus' Names* (Eugene, OR: Harvest House Publishers, 2019), 149.
370 Daniel 1:7.
371 Genesis 17:5.
372 Genesis 32:28.
373 Acts 13:9.
374 2 Samuel 22:4, ESV.
375 Acts 2:21, CSB.
376 2 Kings 6:15, NKJV.
377 2 Kings 6:16, TLB.
378 2 Kings 6:17, NLT.
379 1 John 4:4, BSB.
380 2 Kings 6:16, NCV.
381 1 Samuel 1:11, HCSB.
382 Doctrine and Covenants 84:88.
383 Psalm 9:10, EtRV.
384 *Shabbath* 7.2, Soncino ed. of the Talmud, p. 348, 349.
385 Mark 2:24, NLT.
386 Mark 2:27–28, NLT.
387 Matthew 23:27, NLT.
388 Doctrine and Covenants 78:18.
389 Exodus 31:13-14, 16–17, GNT.
390 1 Peter 5:6; Luke 18:14.
391 1 John 4:16.
392 2 Nephi 2:25.
393 Doctrine and Covenants 19:18.
394 2 Nephi 31:19; Alma 7:14; Alma 34:18; Doctrine and Covenants 133:47.
395 Doctrine and Covenants 110:5; Matthew 25:21; ISV.
396 Mathew 25:21, (ISV)
397 Luke 22:26, CEB.
398 Matthew 6:24, NKJV.
399 Moroni 7:11.
400 Joshua 24:15, NCV.
401 Leviticus 25:55, CEV.
402 Doctrine and Covenants 4:2.
403 Matthew 25:21, MEV.
404 Romans 6:23, KJV.
405 Abraham Booth, *By God's Grace Alone* (London: Grace Publication Trust, 1983), 60–61.
406 Isaiah 1:18, NIV.
407 Galatians 3:13, NLT.
408 Doctrine and Covenants 19:18.
409 John 1:29, NIV.
410 Colossians 1:28, KJV.
411 Romans 6:14, DLNT.
412 Galatians 2:20, NLV.
413 Martin Luther, *Luther's Works, Vol. 27: Lectures on Galatians*, 1535, chapters 5–6; 1519, chapters 1–6, ed. J.

J. Pelikan, H. C. Oswald, and H. T. Lehmann (Saint Louis: Concordia Publishing House, 1999), 13.
414 Daniel K. Judd, W. Justin Dyer "Grace, Legalism, and Mental Health among the Latter-day Saints," *BYU Studies Quarterly—59:1, p. 23.*
415 Moroni 10:32–33.
416 Hebrews 9:15, TLB.
417 Psalm 4:1, GNT.
418 Luke 23:34, CSB.
419 Mosiah 4:2; Helaman 12:7.
420 John 5:30, NCV.
421 Luke 22:42, CSB.
422 Matthew 23:12, GNT.
423 C.H. Spurgeon, "The Meek and Lowly One," A sermon delivered On Sunday, July 31, 1859 at the Royal Surrey Gardens.
424 Alma 38:14.
425 Rich Wilkerson, Jr., *Friend of Sinners* (Nashville, TN: Thomas Nelson, 2018), 17.
426 Luke 14:11, NIV.
427 Matthew 5:3, NLT.
428 Acts 10:38, KJV; Mormon 9:18.
429 John 21:25, GNT.
430 2 Nephi 4:34.
431 Mosiah 4:2; John 15:5, GNT.
432 Matthew 19:26, NIV.
433 Alma 7:14.
434 Jacob 4:7.
435 Ephesians 6:10, ISV.
436 Zephaniah 3:17, GWT.
437 Genesis 1:3, 6, 9.
438 Luke 1:37, NIRV.
439 Matthew 15:30–31, CEV.
440 Luke 1:37, NASB; Genesis 18:14, NCV.
441 Doctrine and Covenants 1:19.
442 John 15:5, CSB.
443 Matthew 23:12, KJV.
444 Doctrine and Covenants 4:2.
445 Job 15:2, NLT.
446 Mosiah 4:2.
447 Mosiah 4:5.
448 Alma 38:14.
449 Mosiah 4:11.
450 Abraham Booth, *By God's Grace Alone* (London: Grace Publication Trust, 1983), 69.
451 Ether 12:27.
452 Luke 1:37, CEV.
453 Philippians 4:13, BSB.
454 2 Corinthians 12:9, NLT.
455 John 1:14, NIV.
456 John 17:21–22, KJV.
457 John 16:15, CSB.
458 Mark 10:8, NIV.
459 Jeff A. Benner, *His Name Is One* (self-published, 2002), 23.
460 Matthew 10:19, NLT.
461 Philippians 4:19, CSB.
462 Exodus 8:1, KJV.
463 Exodus 8:3.
464 Exodus 8:16, KJV.
465 Exodus 9:23.
466 Exodus 12:12, NLT.
467 Exodus 12:13, BSB; Exodus 12:13, ESV.
468 Alma 13:11.
469 Revelations 12:11, KJV.
470 Romans 4:7, NIV.
471 Doctrine and Covenants 45:5.
472 Jeffrey R. Holland, "Be Ye Therefore Perfect—Eventually," General Conference, October 2017.
473 Matthew 5:48, KJV.

474 Daniel K. Judd and W. Justin Dyer, "Grace, Legalism, and Mental Health among the Latter-day Saints," *BYU Studies Quarterly 59:1*, 2020. American Psychological Association, "APA Dictionary of Psychology," Retrieved May 21, 2023 from https://dictionary.apa.org/perfectionism

475 2 Nephi 2:25.

476 Spiros Zodhiates, *The Complete Word Study New Testament* (Chattanooga, TN: AMG International, Inc., 1991), 960.

477 John 8:5, KJV.

478 John 8:7, KJV.

479 3 Nephi 11:11; Ether 12:33; John 3:16–17.

480 2 Nephi 26:24.

481 Moses 1:39.

482 Jeffrey R. Holland, "Be Ye Therefore Perfect—Eventually," General Conference, October 2017.

483 Jeffrey R. Holland, "Be Ye Therefore Perfect—Eventually," General Conference, October 2017.

484 Moroni 10:32.

485 Romans 8:1, NKJV.

486 Mark 5:26, BSB.

487 Mark 5:28, NLT.

488 Mark 5:29, CEV.

489 Mark 5:30–34, NLT.

490 2 Nephi 25:13.

491 Matthew 9:12, CSB, Matthew 9:13, NLT.

492 C.S. Lewis, *Mere Christianity* (New York, NY: Touchstone, 1996), 38–39.

493 Romans 3:10, DBT.

494 Psalm 6:2, NKJV.

495 Matthew 8:3, NLT.

496 Howard W. Hunter, "Reading the Scriptures," *General Conference*, October 1979.

497 Ether 12:27.

498 John 10:29, KJV.

499 Philippians 3:21, ESV.

500 Mark 4:36, BSB.

501 Mark 4:37, CEV.

502 Mark 4:38, NKJV.

503 Mark 4:38, KJV; Mark 4:38, CSB.

504 Mark 4:39, NHEB.

505 "Where Can I Turn for Peace," Hymn 129.

506 Alma 26:6.

507 Philippians 4:7, NIV.

508 Ephesians 2:14, KJV.

509 John 16:33, NIV.

510 Luke 1:79, NIV.

511 John 1:21, NLT.

512 John 1:21, 20, NLT.

513 John 1:22, NLT.

514 John 1:23, PHBT.

515 John 1:29, KJV.

516 John 1:31, NIV.

517 John 1:34, NKJV.

518 John 14:2–4, CSB.

519 John 14:5, BSB.

520 John 14:6, NLT.

521 John 14:2, CSB.

522 John 14:3, New KJV.

523 Doctrine and Covenants 101:54.

524 Doctrine and Covenants 101:54.

525 Psalm 23:6, NLT.

526 John 1:49, KJV.

527 Luke 2:47, KJV.

528 John 3:1.

529 Luke 4:22, KJV.

530 Luke 4:21, KJV.

Whom Say Ye that I Am?

531 John 20:16, NLT.
532 John 20:17, NLT.
533 Luke 8:2, KJV.
534 John 19:25.
535 Matthew 27:61.
536 John 20:17, NIV;l John 20:17 JST, "Hold me not...".
537 Romans 10:9, NLT.
538 Acts 16:15, NLT.
539 Alma 21:7.
540 Titus 2:14, KJV.
541 *Book of Mormon: Gospel Doctrine Teacher's Manual* (Salt Lake City, UT: The Church of Jesus Christ of Latter-day Saints), 26.
542 James 2:10, KJV.
543 Galatians 2:16, NLT.
544 2 Nephi 2:5.
545 2 Nephi 2:6–9.
546 2 Nephi 2:6.
547 2 Nephi 2:3.
548 Doctrine and Covenants 50:41.
549 Jeffrey R. Holland, "Be Ye Therefore Perfect—Eventually," General Conference, October 2017.
550 Isaiah 44:22, TLV.
551 2 Nephi 33:6.
552 Matthew 11:28–29, NASB.
553 Matthew 11:30, KJV.
554 Jeff A. Benner, *His Name Is One* (self-published 2002), 35.
555 Alma 13:16.
556 Isaiah 30:15, TM.
557 John 11:25, KJV.
558 John 11:5, NLT.
559 John 11:11, NLT.
560 John 11:21, GNT.
561 John 11: 23, 25, KJV.
562 John 11:43, NLT.
563 John 11:45, CEV.
564 John 11:24, CSB.
565 Luke 19:9, CEV.
566 Alma 11:45.
567 Romans 6:11, KJV.
568 Isaiah 10:15, NASB.
569 Romans 11:17, NKJV; Romans 11:18, NLT.
570 1 Corinthians 1:27, KJV.
571 Mosiah 16:9.
572 2 Nephi 25:25.
573 2 Nephi 26:33.
574 Matthew 16:15, KJV.
575 Matthew 16:16, KJV.
576 Matthew 16:17, NET; Matthew 16:18, KJV.
577 Daniel 6:26, NHEB.
578 Helaman 5:12.
579 Acts 4:12, KJV.
580 Luke 19:2, NLT.
581 Luke 19:5, CEV.
582 Luke 19:6, NLT.
583 Luke 19:9, HCSB.
584 Gary E. Stevenson, "Your Priesthood Playbook," *General Conference,* April 2019.
585 Luke 19:9, CEV.
586 Jeff A. Benner, *His Name Is One* (self-published, 2002), 91.
587 Acts 16:31, NKJV.
588 Acts 16:31, NKJV.
589 Ether 12:27.
590 2 Nephi 4:34.
591 Philippians 4:13, NLV.
592 2 Corinthians 12:9, TLB.
593 2 Corinthians 12:9–10, TLB.
594 Isaiah 26:4, NIV.
595 Isaiah 26:4, KJV.
596 Isaiah 12:2, NAB.

597 Matthew 7:24–27, TLB.
598 Nick Bilton, "Part of the Daily American Diet, 34 Gigabytes of Data," *The New York Times*, Dec. 9, 2009. Retrieved on April 4, 2023 from https://www.nytimes.com/2009/12/10/technology/10data.html Dec. 9, 2009.
599 Jacob 4:16.
600 Helaman 5:12.
601 Isaiah 28:16, NIV.
602 2 Timothy 2:19, KJV.
603 Matthew 7:24–25, TLB.
604 1 Nephi 2:10.
605 John 15:1, KJV.
606 John 14:30, NLV.
607 Bruce Wilkinson, *Secrets of the Vine* (Sisters, OR: Multnomah Publishers, Inc., 2001), 12–13.
608 John 15:1–11, ESV.
609 John 15:5, ESV & KJV.
610 John 15:5, ESV.
611 John 15:2, ESV.
612 Bruce Wilkinson, *Secrets of the Vine* (Sisters, OR: Multnomah Publishers, Inc., 2001), 33.
613 Bruce Wilkinson, *Secrets of the Vine* (Sisters, OR: Multnomah Publishers, Inc., 2001), 34–35.
614 Bruce Wilkinson, *Secrets of the Vine* (Sisters, OR: Multnomah Publishers, Inc., 2001), 35.
615 John 15:3, ESV.
616 1 Peter 1:3, KJV.
617 John 15:3, ESV.
618 John 15:11, TLB.
619 John 18:37, KJV.
620 Mark 16:15, NLT.
621 Acts 10:39,43, KJV.
622 Acts 1:8, NLT.
623 Luke 24:48, CEV.
624 Matthew 10:32, TLB; Matthew 10:32, NCV; Doctrine and Covenants 93:38.
625 Revelation 1:5, KJV.
626 Revelations 3:14, KJV.
627 Hebrews 13:8, KJV.
628 Doctrine and Covenants 112:28.
629 Doctrine and Covenants 110:5.
630 John 3:16, KJV.
631 Doctrine and Covenants 18:10–11; 1 Nephi 6:4.
632 Psalm 78:4, KJV.
633 Psalm 107:8, KJV.
634 1 Nephi 15:23.
635 1 Nephi 15:24.
636 1 John 5:7, KJV.
637 Tony Evans, *Power of Jesus' Names* (Eugene, OR: Harvest House Publishers, 2019), 221.
638 1 Nephi 11:31, 33.
639 Revelations 19:13, ESV.
640 Helaman 3:29–30.
641 1 Peter 5:8, NLT.
642 2 Nephi 2:27.
643 Zechariah 13:6, KJV.
644 John 21:12–17.
645 Acts 9:15.
646 Alma 36:11–20.
647 Joseph Smith History 1:17.
648 Doctrine and Covenants 10:10

About the Author

Mitchell C. Taylor is a published author. His first book, *Perfect in Christ: The Good News of God's Grace*, was published when he was seventeen years old and has been endorsed by Dr. Susan Easton Black, Dr. John-Hilton III, and the Executive Director of Leading Saints, Kurt Francom. Mitchell served as a full-time missionary in the Honduras Tegucigalpa Mission. Mitchell is currently attending BYU-Idaho studying business and plans to seek a master's degree in theology.